£55

別冊商店建築 59

ヨーロッパのホテル
&そのレストラン

EUROPEAN HOTELS & their restaurants

武藤聖一 編

はじめに 4

デザイナーズ ホテル 5
HOTEL IM WASSERTURM
〈ホテル イム ヴァッサートルム——ドイツ・ケルン〉 6
LA VILLA HOTEL
〈ラ ヴィラ ホテル——フランス・パリ〉 12
HÔTEL ST-JAMES RESTAURANT
〈オテル サン ジェームス レストラン——フランス・ブリャック〉 ... 19

オーベルジュ & シャトー ホテル 25
LE VIEUX MANOIR AU LAC
〈ル ヴュウ マノワ オ ラック——スイス・メイリッツ ムルテン〉 ... 26
HÔTEL SCHLOSS FUSCHL
〈オテル シュロッス フッシェル——オーストリア・ザルツブルグ〉 ... 33
HOTEL PALACIO DE SATEAIS
〈ホテル パラシオ デュ セティス——ポルトガル・シントラ〉 ... 40
OUSTAU DE BAUMANIÈRE
〈ウストウ デュ ボーマニエール——フランス・ル ボー デュ プロバンス〉 ... 47

ニュー インターナショナル ホテル 51
HILTON BARCELONA
〈ヒルトン バルセロナ——スペイン・バルセロナ〉 52
SAS ROYAL HOTEL BRUSSELS
〈サス ロイヤル ホテル ブリュッセル——ベルギー・ブリュッセル〉 ... 58
SAS ROYAL HOTEL AMSTERDAM
〈サス ロイヤル ホテル アムステルダム——オランダ・アムステルダム〉 ... 64
MARITIM HOTEL BONN
〈マリティーム ホテル ボン——ドイツ・ボン〉 70
HOTEL INTER·CONTINENTAL STUTTGART
〈ホテル インター・コンチネンタル——ドイツ・シュトゥットガルト〉 ... 76
HOTEL ARIADNE
〈ホテル アリアードン——スウェーデン・ストックホルム〉 ... 82
SERGEL PLAZA HOTEL
〈セルゲル プラザ ホテル——スウェーデン・ストックホルム〉 ... 89

ヨーロッパのホテル
&そのレストラン
目 次

SCANDIC CROWN HOTEL
〈スカンティック クラウン ホテル——スウェーデン・ウップランズ ヴェスビー〉 ... 95
HEATHROW STERLING HOTEL
〈ヒースロー スターリング ホテル——イギリス・ヒースロー空港〉 ... 101
HOTEL SOFITEL TOULOUSE
〈ホテル ソフィテル トゥロウーズ——フランス・トゥロウーズ〉 ... 108
OSLO PLAZA HOTEL
〈オスロ プラザ ホテル——ノルウェイ・オスロ〉 114
HOTEL STRAND INTER·CONTINENTAL
〈ホテル ストランド インター・コンチネンタル——フィンランド・ヘルシンキ〉 ... 121
STOCKHOLM GLOBE HOTEL
〈ストックホルム グローブ ホテル——スウェーデン・ストックホルム〉 ... 127

トラディショナル ホテル 133
HOTEL RITZ BARCELONA
〈ホテル リッツ バルセロナ——スペイン・バルセロナ〉 ... 134
HOTEL NEGRESCO
〈ホテル ネグレスコ——フランス・ニース〉 142
THE RITZ LONDON
〈ザ リッツ ロンドン——イギリス・ロンドン〉 150
HOLMENKOLLEN PARK HOTEL
〈ホルメンコーレン パーク ホテル——ノルウェイ・オスロ〉 ... 156
COPENHAGEN ADMIRAL HOTEL
〈コペンハーゲン アドミラル ホテル——デンマーク・コペンハーゲン〉 ... 163
BONAPRTE HOTEL
〈ボナパルト ホテル——イタリー・ミラノ〉 169
HÔTEL PLAZA ATHÉNÉE
〈オテル プラザ アテネ——フランス・パリ〉 174
ST. ANDREWS OLD COURSE HOTEL
〈セントアンドリュースオールドコースホテル——イギリス・セントアンドリュース〉 ... 180
THE DORCHESTER
〈ザ ドルチェスター——イギリス・ロンドン〉 187
GRAND HOTEL STOCKHOLM
〈グランド ホテル ストックホルム——スウェーデン・ストックホルム〉 ... 193

Foreword ········· 4

Designers' Hotels ········· 5
HOTEL IM WASSERTUM
⟨Köln, Germany⟩ ········· 6
LA VILLA HOTEL
⟨Paris, France⟩ ········· 12
HÔTEL ST-JAMES RESTAURANT
⟨Bouliac, France⟩ ········· 19

Auberges & Chateau Hotels ········· 25
LE VIEUX MANOIR AU LAC
⟨Meyriez-Murten, Switzerland⟩ ········· 26
HÔTEL SCHLOSS FUSCHL
⟨Salzburg, Austria⟩ ········· 33
HOTEL PALACIO DE SATEAIS
⟨Sintra, Portugal⟩ ········· 40
OUSTAU DE BAUMANIÈRE
⟨Les-Baux-de-Provence, France⟩ ········· 47

New International Hotels ········· 51
HILTON BARCELONA
⟨Barcelona, Spain⟩ ········· 52
SAS ROYAL HOTEL BRUSSELS
⟨Brussels, Belgium⟩ ········· 58
SAS ROYAL AMSTERDAM
⟨Amsterdam, Netherlands⟩ ········· 64
MARITIM HOTEL BONN
⟨Bonn, Germany⟩ ········· 70
HOTEL INTER·CONTINENTAL STUTTGART
⟨Stuttgart, Germany⟩ ········· 76
HOTEL ARIADNE
⟨Stockholm, Sweden⟩ ········· 82
SERGEL PLAZA HOTEL
⟨Stockholm, Sweden⟩ ········· 89

EUROPEAN HOTELS & their restaurants
Contents

SCANDIC CROWN HOTEL
⟨Upplands Väsby, Sweden⟩ ········· 95
HEATHROW STERLING HOTEL
⟨Heathrow Airport, U.K.⟩ ········· 101
HOTEL SOFITEL TOULOUSE
⟨Toulouse, France⟩ ········· 108
OLSO PLAZA HOTEL
⟨Oslo, Norway⟩ ········· 114
HOTEL STRAND INTER·CONTINENTAL
⟨Helsinki, Finland⟩ ········· 121
STOCKHOLM GLOBE HOTEL
⟨Stockholm, Sweden⟩ ········· 127

Traditional Hotels ········· 133
HOTEL RITZ BARCELONA
⟨Barcelona, Spain⟩ ········· 134
HOTEL NEGRESCO
⟨Nice, France⟩ ········· 142
THE RITZ LONDON
⟨London, U.K.⟩ ········· 150
HOLMENKOLLEN PARK HOTEL
⟨Oslo, Norway⟩ ········· 156
COPENHAGEN ADMIRAL HOTEL
⟨Copenhagen, Denmark⟩ ········· 163
BONAPRTE HOTEL
⟨Milano, Italy⟩ ········· 169
HÔTEL PLAZA ATHÉNÉE
⟨Paris, France⟩ ········· 174
ST. ANDREWS OLD COURSE HOTEL
⟨St. Andrews, U.K.⟩ ········· 180
THE DORCHESTER
⟨London, U.K.⟩ ········· 187
GRAND HOTEL STOCKHOLM
⟨Stockholm, Sweden⟩ ········· 193

はじめに

日本人の海外旅行者がすでに、年間で、1,000万人を突破した今日、ビジネスはますます国際化し、旅行も団体による観光から、より個性化にリゾートライフを反映したものへと変化し、豪華さをます傾向が特に著しい。これは日本に限らず、世界的なものと言えよう。こうしたブームに対応して、'80年代を境に、多くのアーバン・スタイルやリゾート・スタイルのホテルが新築され、また、既存のホテルも増改築されたり、内装が一新され同時にサービスも改善され、より充実された。これはヨーロッパに限られたことではないが、こうしたアメニティ性を付加することやコンベンションなどの施設を充実することで、激化するホテル間の競争を退け、売上の安定と増を確保しているのが実情のようだ。

海外に出かける機会が増え、さらに利用しやすくなった今、ホテルは単なる宿泊のための施設としてのみでなく、ライフスタイル、あるいはビジネスのステータスとしてなど、利用目的にあわせて、気安く選択する時期がきたと言っても過言ではないと思う。

本書の取材にあたって、'90年から'91年前半にかけて、西ヨーロッパ十数ケ国のホテルを見てまわったが、各国の生活・文化が複雑、且つ多様化しているのにはあらためて驚かされたと同時に、素晴らしいホテル系列とそのマネージメントに先行されることなく

● 1990年代のホテルインテリアのトレンドをリードする、デザイナーズ ホテル
● 中世ヨーロッパの空間を現代に受け継ぐ、宮殿風・旅籠風のシャトー ホテルとオーベルジュ
● '80～'90年代に建設された、比較的新しいビジネス感覚のニュー インターナショナル ホテル
● 伝統・格式が重んじられている、トラディショナル ホテル

の大きく四つのカテゴリーに分け、ヨーロッパの広範囲から30ケ所をセレクトしたものである。ここで取りあげたホテルの、特色は、インテリア・スタイル・格式など、一応とらえ得たと思う。ホテル空間そのものは、実際に旅をし、訪れ、宿泊していただくのが最良であるが、本書を通じ、誇張されない、ホテルの実感に近い雰囲気を感じていただければ、幸いである。

最後に、撮影・取材に御協力いただいた各ホテル、編集にあたっては、商店建築社の辻田 博氏、レイアウトのぱとおく社の森田 実氏など関係各位に厚く感謝いたします。

1991年11月

武藤聖一
〈フォト ジャーナリスト〉

FOREWORD

The annual number of Japanese people travelling abroad has already topped 10 million, and business activities have been increasingly internationalized. In these circumstances, Japanese travel has also changed in its nature from mere group sight-seeing to a more individualized and luxuriant tour oriented to resort life. This may be said to be a worldwide tendency, not limited to Japan. Reflecting this boom, since the 1980s, many new urban and resort style hotels have been constructed and the existing hotels have been either renovated or expanded with refurbished interiors and improved service in Europe. Although this is not limited to Europe, it seems to be true that by adding amenity features or expanding a convention facility, European hotels are trying to survive severe competition and thereby stabilize/increase sale proceeds.

Now that we have more of a chance of going abroad and hotels have become easier to utilize, it will be no exaggeration to say that the time has come for casually selecting a hotel not merely as a mere facility to stay in, but also according to one's life-style, business status, or for any other purpose.

In order to collect data for the book, I visited some ten odd countries in Western Europe from 1990 to the first half of 1991 to survey hotels there. I was amazed afresh at the complicated and diversified life and culture in those countries, and also came across so many wonderful hotels that I actually had trouble in selecting them. In selecting hotels, without giving priority to either hotel chain or management, 30 hotels have been selected from different parts of Europe as per the following four categories:

- Designers' hotels leading the trend of hotel interiors in the 1990s.
- Palace styled and tavern styled chateau hotels and auberges which have transmitted medieval European spaces to date.
- New international hotels featuring a relatively new business sense constructed in the 1980s and early 1990s.
- Traditional hotels which make much of tradition and status.

The hotels contained in the book are believed to generally represent those characteristic interiors, styles, status, etc. Although a hotel space can be best felt by actually visiting and staying there, I am very pleased if readers feel an atmosphere which is not exaggerated but close to the actual hotel atmosphere.

In closing, let me extend my deep thanks to the hotels which kindly cooperated with me in photographing and collecting data, Mr. Hirosh Tsujita, Shotenkenchikusha, for his help in editing, Mr. Minoru Morita, Patohkusha, for aiding in layout, and many others involved in the publication.

November 1991

Shoichi Muto
Photo Journalist

Published by Shotenkenchiku-sha Co., Ltd.
7-22-36-2, Nishi-shinjuku, Shinjuku-ku, Tokyo
160 Japan

(ⓒ 1991)

All rights reserved. No part of this publication be reproduced without the prior permission on the publisher.

Printed in Japan

別冊商店建築59 ヨーロッパのホテル&そのレストラン 1992年1月31日発行

著者 武藤聖一　編集 辻田 博　協力スタッフ　本文レイアウト●ぱとおく社　印刷●三共グラフィック　製本●坂田製本
編集発行人 村上末吉　制作 菅谷良夫　表紙デザイン●ウィークエンド　英文●海広社　写植●福島写植　山田製本
発行所　株式会社商店建築社ⓒ
本社 東京都新宿区西新宿7-22-36-2　〒160 TEL03(3363)5770代　支社 大阪市中央区西心斎橋1-9-28 第3大京ビル 〒542 TEL06(251)6523代
ISBN：4-7858-0020-8 C2052

Designers' Hotels／デザイナーズ ホテル

HOTEL IM WASSERTURM〈Köln, Germany〉／ホテル イム ヴァッサートルム〈ドイツ, ケルン〉
Add : Kaygasse 2, D-5000 Köln 1 Germany   Phone : 0221-2008-0 6

LA VILLA HOTEL〈Paris, France〉／ラ ヴィラ ホテル〈フランス, パリ〉
Add : 29 Rue Jacob 75006 Paris, France   Phone : 1-43 26 60 00 12

HÔTEL ST-JAMES RESTAURANT〈Bouliac, France〉／オテル サン ジェームス レストラン〈フランス, ブリャック〉
Add : 3 Place Camille-Hostein 33270 Bouliac, France 19

上階からレセプションを俯瞰する　　　　　　　　　　　　　　The reception area overlooked from an upper floor.

Hotel im Wasserturm

Add : Koygasse 2 D-5000 Köln 1, Germany
Phone : 0221-2008-0

屋上にはレストランがある　　　There is a restaurant on the roof.

レセプションの上部　　　　　　　　　　　　　　The upper part of the reception area.

レセプション　　　　　　　　　　　　　　　　　The reception area.

左/給水塔を改装したファサード　デザインはAndrée Putman氏
Left / The facade prepared by redecorating the water tower; designed by Andrée Putman.

屋上のレストラン
The restaurant on the roof.

テーブル セッティングと柱の照明
The table setting and pillar lighting.

入口にあるワイン テーブル
The wine table by the entrance.

ホテル イム ヴァッサートルム

1872年に建造され ヨーロッパで最大規模を誇ったケルンの水道塔は その後市の歴史建造物に指定され 1900年以降はその機能を発揮せずに ワークショップや倉庫に使用されていたが 1990年になり フランスの建築家 アンドレー プットマン(Andrée Putman)の手で 見事にインターナショナルクラスの高級ホテルに生まれ変わった。

建造当時 直径34m 高さ35.5mあったこのブロック造りのこのタワーは 第二次世界大戦で上部が破壊され 27mになっていた。今回の改築に際して ブロック構造を最大限残し 2層部分が増築され 内部を10階のレベルにし 最上階(屋上)はガラス窓の明るいレストランになっている。タワーは採光部分だけが僅かにくり抜かれただけで ほぼ原形をとどめている。エントランス廻りは ガラスのキャノピー(canopy)が設けられ 内部の新しいデザインは そのコントラストを生じながらも 未来空間への橋渡しをしているかのような感がある。

開業/1990年1月 客室数/90室(シングル 10室 ダブル 38室 ジュニア スイート 34室 スイート 8室) 主な施設/サウナ ソラリウム マッサージ

セミ サークル状のバー カウンター
The semicircular bar counter.

HOTEL IM WASSERTURM

Constructed in 1872, the Wasserturm in Köln had been the largest water tower in Europe, but was thereafter designated as the city's historical building. From 1900, however, it was used as a workshop or warehouse. In 1990, however, it was wonderfully renewed by French architect Andrée Putman into a high class hotel of international standing.

Originally, the block-built tower was 34 m in diameter and 35.5 m in height, but during the Second World War its upper part was destroyed so that the height decreased to 27 m. On the occasion of the current reconstruction, the block structure has been almost completely retained and the inner 2-layer space was extended to form 10 floors, including the roof (highest) which is used as a bright restaurant with glass windows. Except for only a small portion removed to introduce light, the tower retains its original shape. The entrance area is provided with a glass canopy, and although the new interior design produces a contrast with the old space, it seems to be guiding the old space to a future space.

Opened/January 1990; Number of rooms/90 (single 10, double 38, junior suite 34, suite 8); Main facilities/sauna, solarium, massage

バー ロビーから奥のバー カウンター方向をみる
The inner bar counter viewed from the bar lobby.

プレジデント スイート ルーム

The president suite room.

ソファーのバックのスクリーンは後ろ側からライティングされる
The screen behind the sofa receives lighting from the rear side.

プレジデント スイート ルームの応接間
The reception room in the president suite room.

プレジデント スイート ルームのベッド ルームから下のソファーを俯瞰する　　The lower sofa overlooked from the bedroom in the president suite room.

ベッド ルーム
The bedroom.

ミラーは開閉できるコンパクトなもの
The compact mirror can be opened/closed.

ファサード　　　　　　　　The facade.

レセプション　　　　　　　The reception.

la villa

Add : 29 Rue Jacob 75006 Paris, France
Phone : 1-43 26 60 00

エントランス ロビー

The entrance lobby.

スイート ルームのリビング　　　　　　　　　　　　　　　　　　　　The living room in the suite room.

スポット照明がこのホテルの特色　　The hotel features spot lighting.

テーブルのデザイン　　　　　　　　The table design.

ベッド ルーム　天井のデザインがおもしろい　　The bedroom; with the interesting ceiling design.

上・下/ドアの把っ手
Top・bottom/The door knob.

各ルーム前にはスポットライトでルームナンバーを表現している
Spot lights before each room express the room number.

トイレット ブース　　　　　　　　　　　　　　The toilet booth.

15

ラ ヴィラ ホテル

パリの左岸(Rive Gauche)の最もパリらしい雰囲気を残すサンジェルマン デ プレ(Saint Germain des Prés)周辺は カフェ ファッション ブティック ギャラリーなどが集まり 常に賑わいを見せているところ。パリで最も古いサンジェルマン デ プレ教会(Eglise Saint Germain des Prés)横のヤコブ通り(Rue Jacob)に 四ツ星ホテル「La Villa」がオープンし 1990年代のホテル インテリアの方向をうちだすものとしてセンセーショナルであった。レセプション バー 各部屋の照明 家具 トイレット ブース ドア ノブに至るまで インテリアのすべてを女性デザイナー マリー クリスティーヌ ドルネー(Marie Christine Dorner)が手掛けている。皮 メタル プレーン ウッド ガラスなどの素材を駆使したオリジナルものであり 女性らしい優美で洗練されたタッチと そのコンポジションは見事である。1991年には 地階に新しくジャズ クラブがオープンし(これは彼女のデザインではないが)界隈の新しい社交場として人気を得ている。

開業/1989年3月
客室/31室(内 スイート 4室)

LA VILLA HOTEL

Saint Germain des Prés on Rive Gauche retains the most Parisian atmosphere, and the area, where cafés, fashion boutiques, galleries, etc. are centered, is always bustling. The 4-star hotel "La Villa" opened on Rue Jacob beside Eglise Saint Germain des Prés, the oldest church in Paris, causing a sensation as its interior was felt to point to a new direction in which hotels in the 1990's should turn. The reception, bar, room lighting, furniture, toilet booths, and door knobs — every piece of interior was designed by female designer Marie Christine Dorner. All are her originals made by using materials such as leather, metal, plane wood and glass — their feminine, graceful and refined touch and composition are wonderful. In 1991 a jazz club opened in the basement (which was not designed by her), and is gaining popularity as a new social meeting place in the area.

Opened/March 1989;　Number of rooms/31 (including suite 4)

右上/バー全景
右下/ジャズクラブのステージ

Right, top / The entire bar scene.
Right, bottom / The stage of jazz club.

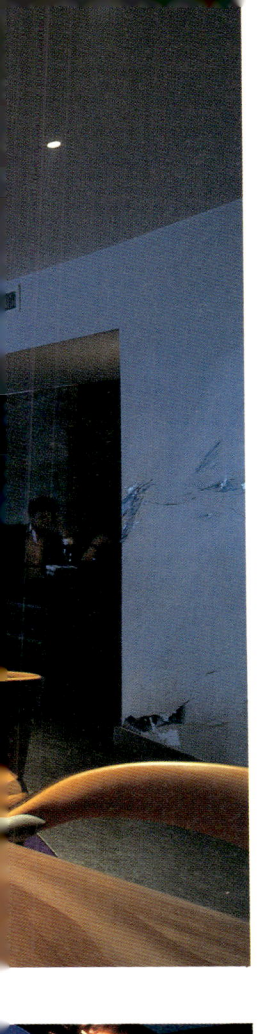

バー カウンター デザイン/Marie Christine Dorner　　The bar counter design/Marie Christine Dorner.

壁面サイドのテーブルと照明
The wall side table and lighting.

バー カウンター
The bar counter.

左/テーブルのディテール
Left / The table in details.

地階のジャズクラブからバーを見上げる

The bar overlooked from the underground jazz club.

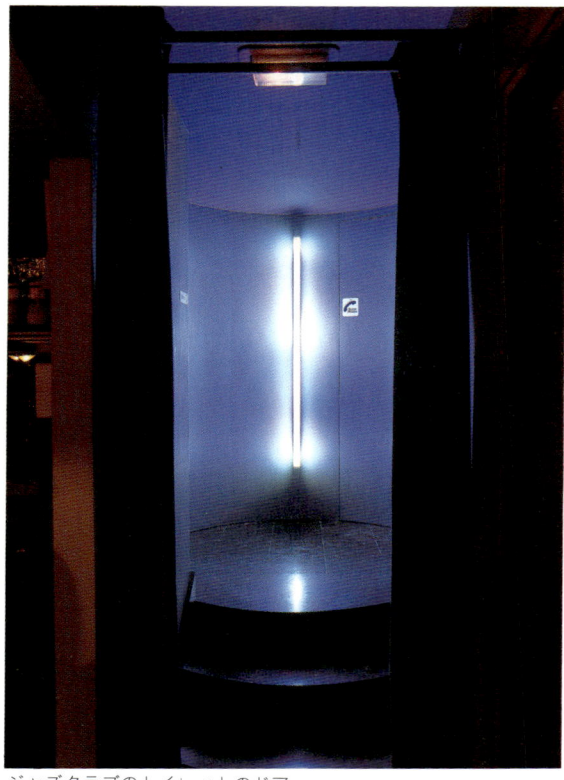

2F PLAN

1F PLAN

ジャズクラブのトイレットのドア
The door of the jazz club's toilet.

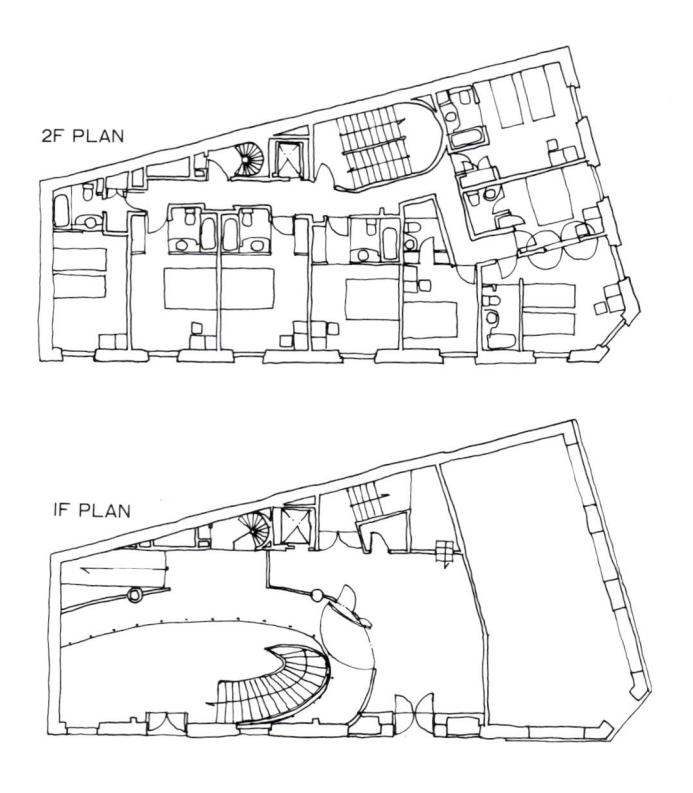

グレージングの格子戸を跳ね上げたホテル棟のコーナー部を見上げる　　　　A corner area of the hotel building where its graded lattice door is raised.

HÔTEL ST-JAMES RESTAURANT
Add : 3 Place Camille-Hostein 33270 Bouliac, France

オテル サン ジェームス レストラン

ボルドー(Bordeaux)市から10k程はなれたガローヌ(Garonne)河右岸の小高い丘の上のブリャック(Bouliac)村に 1989年秋 スパイシーなホテル「St-James」がオープンした。ここは以前 グラン シェフとして名高いジャン マリー アーマット(Jean-Marie Amat)が経営する 17世紀のワイン農園風オーベルジュ(auberges)として人気があったところである。設計はガラスとアルミニュームのオベリスク風のファサードにハイテクを駆使した パリのセーヌ(Seine)河畔のアラブ文化研究所(Institut du Monde Arabe)で注目をあびた ジャン ヌーベル(Jean Nouvel)。ホテルは大きさの異なる4つの棟から成り 後部がオープンの回廊になっており 各棟が結ばれている。

建物の外部は 全面が赤茶色のサビ加工されたグレーチングによって覆われていて 窓の部分のパネルは ガススプリングで外側に跳ね上げられるようになっている。外観は周囲の自然にマッチするよう考慮され 心憎いばかりである。各部屋からは 葡萄畑越しに 谷間に広がるボルドーとガローヌ河が眺望でき 朝の目覚めは 他では味わえない爽快さが約束されている。

開業/1989年11月　客室数/18室

HÔTEL ST-JAMES RESTAURANT

In the fall of 1989 a spicy hotel – "St-James" – opened in Bouliac Village on a small hill on the right bank of the River Garonne which is about 10 km away from Bordeaux City. Formerly, it was a popular auberges with a 17th century winery atmosphere operated by Jean-Marie Amat, a well known grand chef. Designed by Jean Nouvel who drew attention for the Institut du Monde Arabe on the Seine riverside, as it was designed by fully employing high tech in the obelized aluminum facade. The hotel consists of four buildings which differ in size but are linked through an open rear corridor.

The building exterior is covered with rusted red brown grating, and the window panels can be sprung up outward by a gas spring. The appearance is arranged so that it matches the surrounding nature admirably. From each room, across a vineyard, one can command a view of Bordeaux and River Garonne spreading through a valley, and when getting up in the morning, one can feel refreshed more than in any other place.

Opened/November 1989;　Number of rooms/18

葡萄畑から新築のアネックス(4棟)をみる　　The new annexes (4) viewed from a vineyard.

左／オーベルジュのエントランスとガーデン
上／長いコリドールをみる　中央がレセプション
Left / The auberge's entrance and garden.
Top / The long corridor; with the reception in the center.

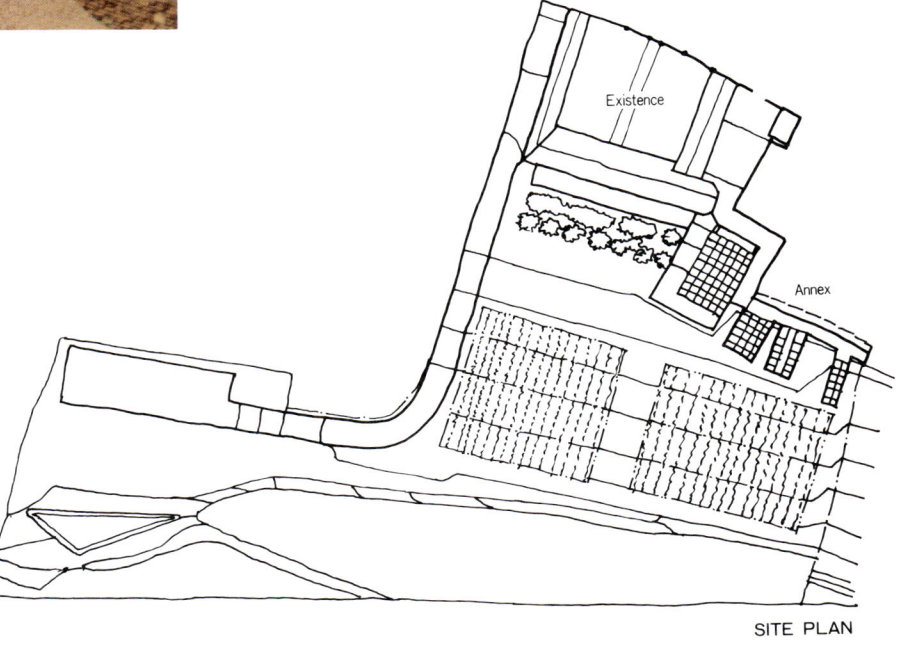

アネックス　　　　　　　　The annex.

SITE PLAN

1階レストラン　窓際からの眺望
The 1st floor restaurant; a view from the window side.

レストランの犬走りから店内をみる
The interior viewed from a scarcement of the restaurant.

厨房からレストラン方向をみる
The restaurant area viewed from the kitchen.

窓際コーナーからレストラン全景をみる　　The entire restaurant scene viewed from a corner by the window.

ホテル側の入口からレストランをみる
The restaurant viewed from the hotel's entrance.

エントランス（ガーデン）左側にあるブラッスリー
The brasserie on the left side of the entrance (garden).

23

ベッドルームからの眺望

A view from the bedroom.

バス ルームからベッド ルームをみる

The bedroom viewed from the bathroom.

上/ベッド ルームからバス ルームをみる
下/日本的にベッドをふとんの高さにした部屋もある

Top / The bathroom viewed from the bedroom.
Bottom / A room where the bed is placed at a level as low as bedclothes in Japanese style.

Auberges & Chateau Hotels／オーベルジュ＆シャトー ホテル

LE VIEUX MANOIR AU LAC〈Meyriez Murten, Switzerland〉／ル ヴュゥ マノワ オ ラック〈スイス, メイリッツ ムルテン〉
Add：CH-3280 Meyriez Murten, Switzerland　　Phone：037 94 20 26　　　　　　　　　　26

HÔTEL SCHLOSS FUSCHL〈Salzburg, Austria〉／ホテル シュロッス フッシェル〈オーストリア, ザルツブルク〉
Add：A-5322 Hof Bei Salzburg, Austria　　Phone：06229-22530　　　　　　　　　　33

HOTEL PALACIO DE SATEAIS〈Sintra, Portugal〉／ホテル パラシオ デュ セティス〈ポルトガル, シントラ〉
Add：Rua Barbosa do Bocage 2710 Sintra, Portugal　　Phone：9233200　　　　　　　　　　40

OUSTAU DE BAUMANIÈRE〈Les Baux-de-Provence, France〉／ウストウ デュ ボーマニエール〈フランス, ル ボー デュ プロバンス〉
Add：13520 Les Baux-de-Provence, France　　Phone：90 54 33 07　　　　　　　　　　47

広いガーデンのあるオーベルジュ

LE VIEUX MANOIR AU LAC

Add　：CH-3280 Meyriez-Murten, Switzerland
Phone：037-94 20 26

ディレクターのトーマス（Thomas）氏
Mr. Thomas, director.

現在スイート ルームとなっているタワー
The tower which is currently used as a suite room.

エントランス廻り   The entrance area.

The auberge with a wide garden.

サイン   The sign.

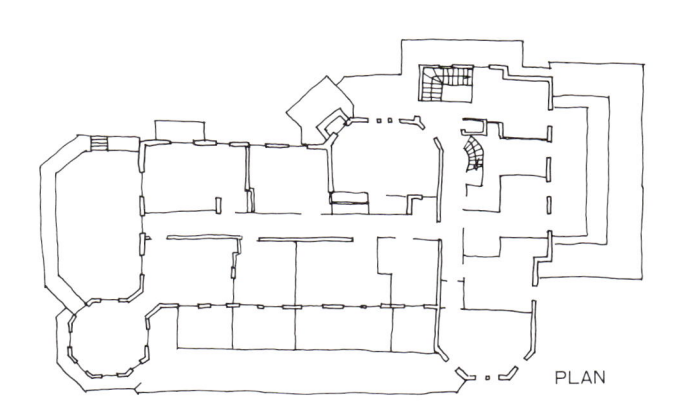

PLAN

27

ロビーへのアプローチ

An approach to the lobby.

ル ヴュゥ マノア オ ラック

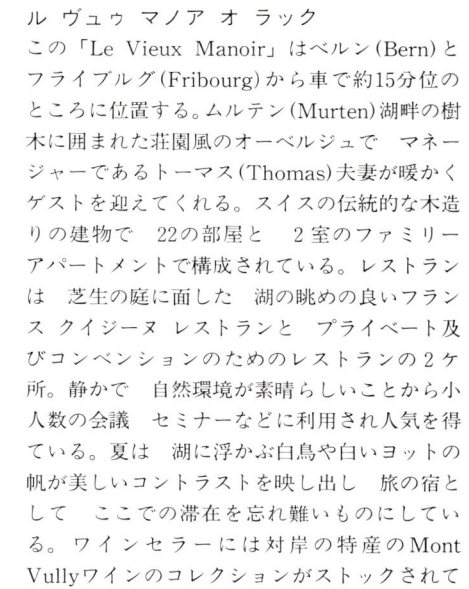

この「Le Vieux Manoir」はベルン（Bern）とフライブルグ（Fribourg）から車で約15分位のところに位置する。ムルテン（Murten）湖畔の樹木に囲まれた荘園風のオーベルジュで マネージャーであるトーマス（Thomas）夫妻が暖かくゲストを迎えてくれる。スイスの伝統的な木造りの建物で 22の部屋と 2室のファミリー アパートメントで構成されている。レストランは 芝生の庭に面した 湖の眺めの良いフランス クイジーヌ レストランと プライベート及びコンベンションのためのレストランの2ケ所。静かで 自然環境が素晴らしいことから小人数の会議 セミナーなどに利用され人気を得ている。夏は 湖に浮かぶ白鳥や白いヨットの帆が美しいコントラストを映し出し 旅の宿として ここでの滞在を忘れ難いものにしている。ワインセラーには対岸の特産のMont Vullyワインのコレクションがストックされている。

客室数/22室（別に ファミリー アパートメント 2室あり）

ロビー ラウンジとチーズ ボード　　The lobby lounge and cheese board.

LE VIEUX MANOIR AU LAC

Situated at a location about 15 minutes by car away from Berne and Fribourg, "Le Vieux Manoir Au Lac" is an auberges like a manor surrounded with trees by Lake Murten. Mr. Thomas the manager, and his wife warmly welcome guests. It is a traditional wooden Swiss building composed of 22 rooms and 2 family apartments. One of the two restaurants serves French cuisine and faces a lawn garden and commands a fine view of the lake, and the other restaurant is for private and convention use. Since the natural environment is wonderful, it is gaining popularity as a place for small members to meet, seminars, etc. In summer, the swans and the white yacht sailing beautifully, contrast with the lake, making ones stay at the hotel unforgettable to travellers. In the wine cellar a collection of local Mont Vully wine – grown on the opposite side of the lake – is stocked.

Number of rooms/22 (2 family apartments are also available.)

レセプション脇の２階への階段　　The staircase beside the reception leading to the 2nd floor.

西側のレストラン
The western restaurant.

サマー用のテラス席
The terrace seating area for summer season.

窓際の席　ブルーのテーブルクロスが鮮やか
The window side seating area; accented with a vividly blue tablecloth.

レストラン サロン　　　　　　　　　　　　　　　　　　　　　　　　　　　　　　　　The restaurant's salon.

ベッド サイドから窓とカーテンをみる

The window and curtain viewed from the bed side.

リビングからベッド ルームをみる
The bedroom viewed from the living room.

トイレット ブース

The toilet booth.

15世紀には　ザルツブルグ大司教の狩猟用の屋敷で　フッシェル(Fuschl)湖に面している
In the 15th century the building was a mansion by the archbishop of Salzburg for hunting, and it faces Lake Fuschl.

ロッジ下のデコレーション
Decoration under the lodge.

ベランダの花々がいかにもオーストリア的
Flowers on the verandah are quite Austrian.

Hotel Schloß Fuschl

Add : A-5322 Hof-Bei Salzburg, Austria
Phone : 06229-22530

各ルームに続く階段廻り

以前セーラーであった城の地下を利用したプール
The pool made by utilizing an underground space of the castle which was formerly a cellar.

上/会議室
下/レセプション
Top / The conference room.
Bottom / The reception.

The staircase area leading to each room.

35

サロン

The salon.

キャッスルのホールにあるバー

The bar in the castle's hall.

ホテル シュロッス フッシェル

ザルツブルグ(Salzburg)市内から東へ約19K フッシェル(Fuschl)湖に面した半島に位置するこのホテルの歴史は エキサイトしていた15世紀のルネッサンス期に溯のぼる。この建物は当時ザルブルグ大司教の狩猟用の屋敷として使用されていたもので 1948年にホテル レストランに改装 さらに1977年にコンベンションセンター ヘルス ビューティサロンなどを増築し 従業員200人を有するオーストリアで最も豪華なリゾート ホテルへと変身した。冬はスキー スケート 夏は水上スキー テニス フィッシング ウインド サーフィン ゴルフ ライフル射撃などの施設が完備され 四季を問わず 贅沢なリゾート ライフが満喫できる。湖ごしに スイス アルプスを眺めを楽しみながら地元でとれた新鮮な鮭や鱒の料理を食べるのも又格別である。

開業/1948年 客室数/90室 主な施設とスポーツ/コンベンション センター(Waldhaus－300人収容) 室内プール ソラリウム サウナ マッサージ プライベート ビーチ サーフィン レンタル ボート ライフル シューティング レンジ(50m) テニス ゴルフ 乗馬 ほか

HÔTEL SCHLOSS FUSCHL

Situated on a peninsula facing Lake Fuschl which is about 19 km east of Salzburg, the hotel dates back to the Renaissance in the 15th century when people were exciting. In those days, the building was used as a mansion by the archbishop of Salzburg for hunting. In 1948 it was renovated into a hotel & restaurant, and in 1977 it was additionally provided with a convention center, health beauty salon, etc., thus changing into the most gorgeous resort hotel in Austria having 200 employees.

Since the hotel is fully equipped with a variety of leisure facilities, guests can enjoy a luxurious resort life in all seasons – skiing and skating in winter, water-skiing, tennis, fishing, windsurfing, golf, rifle shooting, etc. in the summer and other seasons. It is also wonderful to eat dishes cooked by using fresh local salmon and trout, while viewing the Swiss Alps across the lake.

Opened/1948; Number of rooms/90; Main facilities and sports/convention center (Waldhaus: accommodating 300 persons), indoor pool, solarium, sauna, massage, private beach, surfing, rental boat, rifle shooting range (50 m), tennis, golf, riding, etc.

上・下/スイートのダイニング ルーム
Top・bottom / The dining room in the suite room.

ベッド メーキング
Bed making.

スイートルームのフルーツ
Fruits in the suite room.

上・左下/テラス レストラン フッシェル湖と遠くにスイス アルプスを望む

テーブル セッティング(ランチ タイム)
Table setting (at lunchtime).

レストラン

The restaurant.

Top・left, bottom / The terrace restaurant; commanding a view of Lake Fuschl and Swiss Alps in the distance.

大きな窓からの眺めは一枚の絵のように美しい
The large window is beautiful like a scroll of picture.

広い芝生のガーデンのあるホテル / The hotel with a spacious grassed garden.

ガーデンのプールを通して遠く大西洋を望む
Commanding a view of the Atlantic Ocean in the distance across the garden pool.

プール サイドのバーテンダー
A bartender by the poolside.

Hotel Palácio de Seteais

Add : Rua Barbosa do Bocage 2710 Sintra, Portugal
Phone : 9233200

ホテルのゲート　　　　　　　　　　　The hotel gate.

ドリンク　　　　　　　　Drinks.

ホテル パラシオ デュ セティズ

壮麗な18世紀の宮殿建築の一例を見せる「ホテル パラシオ デュ セディス」は リスボンの西側約25Kの古都シントラ(Sintra)の ポルトガルの稜線と大西洋を見渡す高台にある。この宮殿は 当時リスボン在住のオランダ領事によって建造されたもので その後マリアルヴァの5代目侯爵(Fifth Marquis of Marialva)が買い取り 隣りにアーチ及び対称の建物を建て 西側にはフランス庭園を設けた。以後 上流階級の華やかなパーティ会場になっていた。現在はチボリホテル系列の5つ星ホテルで 調度品をはじめ サロン バー レストランなど随所に描かれた フリータッチのペイントが空間内にリズミカルな快感を与えている。アーチ越しに東の山頂に見えるペナの宮殿(Palace of Pena)も素晴らしい。

ゲートを通してペナ宮殿(Palace of Pena)をみる　　The Palace of Pena viewed through the gate.

HOTEL PALACIO DE SATEAIS

An example of a magnificent palace building in the 18th century, the "HOTEL PALACIO DE SATEAIS" stands on a hill in the ancient city Sintra about 25 km west of Lisbon, overlooking the ridges of Portugal and the Atlantic Ocean. The building was originally constructed by the Dutch consul residing in Lisbon in those days, and thereafter purchased by the Fifth Marquis of Marialva who installed an adjacent arch and symmetrical building, and also a French garden on the west side. Since then, it had been used as a luxurious party hall for high society. At present, it is a 5-star hotel belonging to the Tivoli Hotel chain, and the interior space is rhythmically accented with utensils, and free-touch painting drawn here and there in the salon, bar, restaurant, etc. Across the arch one can command a wonderful view of the Palace of Pena on an eastern mountain top.

きれいにペイントされたサロン　　　　　　　　　　　　　　　　　　　　　　　　　　The beautifully painted salon.

ギャラリーから階段廻りをみる　　The staircase area viewed from the gallery.

上/裏庭に出られるトンネル状の廊下　ここから大西洋がみえる
下/レセプション
Top / The tunnel-like corridor from which one can step into the back garden; from the corridor one can command a view of the Atlantic.
Bottom / The reception.

ロビー横のロイヤル サロン　　　　　　　　　　　　　　　　　　　　　　　　　　　　　The royal salon beside the lobby.

ガーデンに面したバー　　　　　　The bar facing the garden.

ロビーから続くギャラリー
The gallery continuing from the lobby.

43

豪華な雰囲気のレストラン

レストランの窓側コーナー　A window-side corner in the restaurant.

美しいテーブル セッティング　The beautiful table setting.

The restaurant having a gorgeous atmosphere.

上・下/客室棟のグランド サロン　　　　　　　　　　Top・bottom / The grand salon in the guest room building.

上・左/シングル ルーム　　　　　　Top・left / The single room.

白い石灰岩の露出した山塊を背にして建つ最高級オーベルジュ
The highest class auberge standing against a mass of mountains with white exposed limestone.

ドリンク　　　　　　　　　Drinks.

春先のガーデン　　　　　　The garden in the early spring.

OUSTAU DE BAUMANIÈRE
Add　: 13520 Les Baux de Provence, France
Phone : 90 54 33 07

トンネル状のロビー　後方はレセプション

The tunnel-like lobby; the reception is visible behind.

ロビー　キャンドルや暖炉がムードをもり上げている

The lobby; accented with the candlelight and fireplace cheer up the mood.

オーベルジュ内にあるショップのファサード　The facade of the shop in the auberge.

ウストゥ デュ ボーマニエール

アヴィニヨン(Avignon)からマルセイユ(Marseilles)にかけては 茶褐色の石灰岩が露出したプロヴァンス(Provins)地方特有の山塊が続き 風化された感傷的な風景が展開している。西側のアルル(Arles)からル ボー(Les Baux)にかけては観光コースになっており 週末ドライブに出かける人も多い。この「Oustau de Baumanière」は ル ボーの谷間にあるオーベルジュで 昔からフランス クイジーヌの最高位にランクされている。グラン シェフ レイモンド チュリエール(Raymond Thuilier)さんが創設して以来 グルメ通に人気を博し 現在は孫にあたるジャン アンドレ シャリアル(Jean-André Charial)の腕前に魅せられてはるばるここを訪れる固定客も多いという。邸内には起伏を利用して宿泊施設があり レストランの前にはプールもある。この地方の特産品のラベンダーの香水や テキスタイル クラフト商品 ワインなどを販売するショップもある。

OUSTAU DE BAUMANIÈRE

From Avignon to Marseilles a mass of mountains with exposed brown limestone which are local to Provins ranges, and weathered sentimental scenes continue. From Arles to Les Baux on the western side there is a tourist course which is used by many weekenders for driving.
"Oustau de Baumanière" is an auberge in the Les Baux valley, and has been ranked No. 1 for its French cuisine since olden times. Since it was founded by grand chef Raymond Thuilier, it has been highly rated by gourmets. At present, charmed by the excellent cooking skill of the present chef Jean-André Charial, grandson of the founder, many clients are said to visit it from distance places. Within the residence there is a hotel facility built by utilizing undulations, and there also is a pool in front of the restaurant. There also is a shop selling lavender perfume which is a speciality of this district along with textiles, craft goods, wine, etc.

左上・左下/ショップのインテリア
Left, top・left, bottom / The shop's interior.

上・左下/フランス料理レストラン　フランス クイジーヌの最高位にランクされる グラン シェフ　Raymond Thuilierがオープンした。
Top・left, bottom / French restaurant ranked among the highest French cuisine; opened by Raymond Thuilier, grand chef.

テーブル セッティング　　　　　Table setting.

New International Hotels／ニュー インターナショナル ホテル

HILTON BARCELONA〈Barcelona, Spain〉／ヒルトン バルセロナ〈スペイン、バルセロナ〉
Add : Avenida Diagonal 589-591, Barcelona, Spain　　Phone : 93-4192233 52

SAS ROYAL HOTEL BRUSSELS〈Brussels, Belgium〉／サス ロイヤル ホテル ブリュッセル〈ベルギー、ブリュッセル〉
Add : Wolvengracht 47, B-1000 Brussels, Belgium　　Phone : 2-2192828 58

SAS ROYAL HOTEL AMSTERDAM〈Amsterdam, Netherlands〉／サス ロイヤル ホテル アムステルダム〈オランダ、アムステルダム〉
Add : Rusland 17, 1012 CK Amsterdam, Netherlands　　Phone : 20-231231 64

MARITIM HOTEL BONN〈Bonn, Germany〉／マリティーム ホテル ボン〈ドイツ、ボン〉
Add : Godesberger Allee, 5300 Bonn 2, Germany　　Phone : 0228-81080 70

HOTEL INTER·CONTINENTAL STUTTGART〈Stuttgart, Germany〉／ホテル インター・コンチネンタル シュトゥットガルト〈ドイツ、シュトゥットガルト〉
Add : Neckarstrasse 60, 7000 Stuttgart 1, Germany　　Phone : 0711-2020-0 76

HOTEL ARIADNE〈Stockholm, Sweden〉／ホテル アリアードン〈スウェーデン、ストックホルム〉
Add : Södra Kajen 37, 10052 Stockholm, Sweden　　Phone : 08-6657800 82

SERGEL PLAZA HOTEL〈Stockholm, Sweden〉／セルケル プラザ ホテル〈スウェーデン、ストックホルム〉
Add : Brunkebergstorg 9, Box 16411, 10327 Stockholm, Sweden　　Phone : 08-226600 89

SCANDIC CROWN HOTEL〈Upplands Väsby, Sweden〉／スカンディック クラウン ホテル〈スェーデン、ウップランドヴェスビー〉
Add : Kanalvägen 10, 19461 Upplands Väsby, Sweden　　Phone : 0760-95510 95

HEATHROW STERLING HOTEL〈Heathrow Airport, U.K.〉／ヒースロー スターリング ホテル〈イギリス、ヒースロー空港〉
Add : Terminal 4, Heathrow Airport, Hounslow Middlesex, U.K.　　Phone : 081-7597755 ... 101

HOTEL SOFITEL TOULOUSE〈Toulouse, France〉／ホテル ソフィテル トゥローウズ〈フランス、トゥローウズ〉
Add : 84 Allées Jean-Jaurès, 3100 Toulouse, France　　Phone : 61-10 23 10 108

OSLO PLAZA HOTEL〈Oslo, Norway〉／オスロ プラザ ホテル〈ノルウェイ、オスロ〉
Add : Sonja Henies pl, 3. N-0107 Oslo, Norway　　Phone : 02-171000 114

HOTEL STRAND INTER·CONTINENTAL〈Helsinki, Finland〉／ホテル ストランド インター・コンチネンタル〈フィンランド、ヘルシンキ〉
Add : John Stenbergin Ranfa 4, 00530 Helsinki, Finland　　Phone : 90-39351 121

STOCKHOLM GLOBE HOTEL〈Stockholm, Sweden〉／ストックホルム グローブ ホテル〈スウェーデン、ストックホルム〉
Add : Box 10004, 12126 Stockholm-Globen, Sweden　　Phone : 08-7259000 127

外観
The appearance.

BARCELONA
HILTON

Add : Avenida Diagonal 589-591, Barcelona, Spain
Phone : 93-4192233

エントランス前に立つポーター
A porter standing before the entrance.

4階からラウンジの吹抜

右/ラウンジの吹抜けを見上げる
Right / Looking up at the lounge stairwell.

俯瞰する　　　　　　　　　　　　　　　　　　　The stairwell in the lounge overlooked from the 4th floor.

左/ロビー バー
Left / The lobby bar.

ロビー ラウンジのエレベーター廻り / The elevator area on the lobby lounge.

レセプション / The reception.

エントランスからロビー ラウンジをみる / The lobby lounge viewed from the entrance.

スイート ルームのリビング　　　　　　　　　　The living room in the suite room.

サロン　　　　　　　　The salon.

ベッド ルーム　　　　　　The bedroom.

レストラン　バックのガラス窓には水を流している

The restaurant; water flows down the glass window at the back.

天井の照明にはグリーンを絡ませている

The ceiling lighting is accented with a green tint.

ヒルトン バルセロナ

オリンピックブームに沸くバルセロナ市の 比較的新しい街 アヴェダ ディアニョール (Avenida Diagonal)通りに「Hilton Barcelona」がオープンした。オフィス バー ブティック 高級アパートなどが多い商業地区に位置するこのホテルのファサードは 左右がダーク グレイとホワイトのコントラストになっており ひときわ鮮やかに見える。正面入口には 高いキャノピーがあり 両サイドには浅い噴水池とレストランがある。4階まではアトリウムとなっており その空間内がロビー バーで ホテルのミーティング ポイントになっている。ロビー右奥には「レストラン クリスタル」や 海の幸やフルーツが豊富なカタルーニヤ (Cataluna)風のビュッフェ レストランなどがある。国際的都市としてのホスト的立場を考慮して バンケットやミーティング ルームも充実させている。
客室数/290室 主な施設/ボール ルーム(バンケット750人 レセプション800人 会議1,000人各収容) ヘルス クラブ サウナ

レストランの中央部にあるガラスのオブジェ ハロゲンランプを内蔵している
The glass objet in the center of the restaurant; with a built-in halogen lamp.

エントランス際にあるビュッフェ
The buffet beside the entrance.

HILTON BARCELONA

"Hilton Barcelona" opened on Avenida Diagonal, a relatively new street in Barcelona which is booming with the coming of the Olympics. The hotel is situated on a commercial quarter dense with offices, bars, boutiques, high-class apartment houses, etc., and its facade stands out contrasting its dark grey and white on the left and right sides. The front entrance has a high canopy, and there is a shallow fountain pond and restaurant on both sides. The atrium occupies the space up to the 4th floor and within the space there is a lobby bar which serves as a meeting point in the hotel. On the inner right area of the lobby there are "Restaurants" such as "Restaurant Crystal" and a Catalonian buffet restaurant which serves a variety of marine delicacies and fruits. As an international city, Barcelona must serve as the host of the coming Olympics so that the hotel has been fully equipped with banquet and meeting rooms.

Number of rooms/290; Main facilities/ballroom (banquet/750 persons, reception/800, conference/1,000, health club, sauna.

上・右下／古風な壁に囲まれたガーデン ロビー　　　　　　　　Top・right, bottom / The garden lobby surrounded with old-fashioned walls.

外観夜景　　A night view of the appearance.

SAS Royal Hotel BRUSSELS

Add　 : Godesberger Allee, 5300 Bonn 2, Germany
Phone : 0228-81080

ガーデン ロビーを俯瞰する

Overlooking the garden lobby.

サス ロイヤル ホテル ブリュッセル

ヨーロッパの首都 ブリュッセルにふさわしい「SAS Royal Hotel Brussels」が 1990年1月にオープンした。観光客で賑わうグラン パレ (Grand Palais)やショッピング ギャラリー そして中央駅にも近い古い商業的 文化的な中心街の一画に位置している。アール デコ (Art Deco)スタイルのファサードは ベルギーの建築家Michel Jaspersのインスピレーションでデザインされたもの。トータルで281室のホテルは2階がイタリアン スタイル 3・4階はオリエンタル スタイル 5階スカンジナビア スタイル 6・7階 ロイヤル クラブ (Royal Club)とそれぞれ区別されているのが特徴である。レセプション ロビー裏はアトリウム形式になっており ガーデンが設けられ その一部には 12世紀に建造されたローマ風の城壁が残されている。8階のコーナーには「Rotonde」というボード ルームがあり 市内の眺望が素晴らしい。

開業/1990年1月 客室数281室(内 Royalスイート 5室 アパートメント スイート 4室 エグゼクティブ ジュニアスイート 16室) 各室にビデオ チェックアウト (Video-checkout) テレフォン メッセージ レコーダー付 主な施設/宴会 会議室 バンケット ルーム 14室(最高500人収容) フィットネス センター (300m²) SAS Air Lineチェック イン カウンター

SAS ROYAL HOTEL BRUSSELS

"SAS Royal Hotel Brussels" opened in January 1990; it is a hotel quite becoming to Brussels, the metropolis of Europe, and is situated at a corner of an old central commercial/cultural street which is close to the Grand palais and a shopping gallery crowded with tourists, and also to the central station. An art deco style facade was designed with the inspiration of Belgian architect Michel Jaspers. Having a total of 281 rooms, the hotel is characterized by differently styled floors – i.e. the 2nd floor is in Italian style, the 3rd and 4th floors in Oriental style, the 5th floor in Scandinavian style, and the 6th and 7th floors as the Royal Club. There is an atrium space with a garden behind the reception and lobby, and at a corner a Roman rampart built in the 12th century is preserved. At a corner of the 8th floor there is a boardroom called the "Rotonde" from which one can command a wonderful view of the city.

Opened/January 1990; Number of rooms/281 (including 5 suites, 4 apartment suites, and 16 executive junior suites), each room features a video-checkout and telephone message recorder; Main facilities/ 14 banquet and conference rooms (accommodating up to 500 persons), fitness center (300 m²), SAS Air Line checkin counter.

1階（レセプション フロア）のバー

The bar on the 1st floor (reception floor).

バンケット ルーム

The banquet room.

レセプション / The reception.

最上階にある会議室 / The conference room on the highest floor.

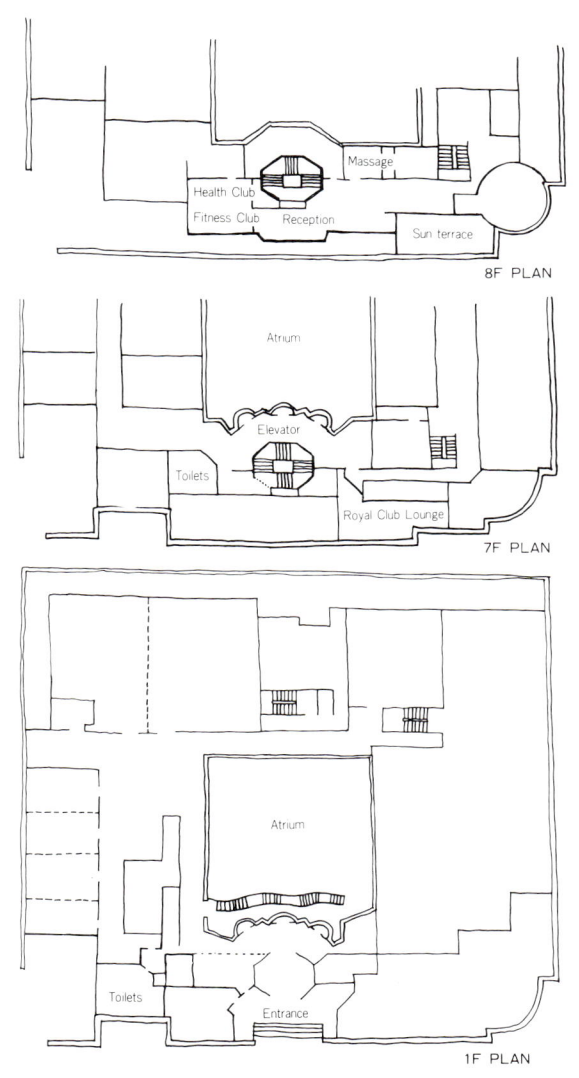

8F PLAN

7F PLAN

1F PLAN

上・左下／「Sea Grill」レストラン　　　　　　　　　　　　　Top・left, bottom / The restaurant "Sea Grill."

サイン　　　　　　　　　　　　　The sign.

イタリアン スタイル ルーム

Italian styled room.

ロイヤル クラブ スイート

The royal club suite.

廊下の窓越しにアトリウムを俯瞰する　　　　　　　　　　　　　Overlooking the atrium through a window along the corridor.

SAS Royal Hotel
AMSTERDAM

Add : Rusland 17, 1012 CK Amsterdam, Netherlands
Phone : 20-231231

64

ロビーを通してレセプションをみる　The reception viewed across the lobby.

上／北棟ファサード
下／南棟ファサード
Top / The North Wing's facade.
Bottom / The South Wing's facade.

北棟と南棟を結ぶ地下通路　The underground aisle connecting the North Wing and the South Wing.

エントランス前に立つドアマン
A doorman standing before the entrance.

サーモン&ステーキ レストラン「Laxenoxen」　　　　The salmon & steak restaurant "Laxenoxen."

デンマーク風オープンサンドイッチ レストラン「Palmboom」　　　　The Danish open sandwich restaurant "Palmboom."

バー「De Pastorie」の奥側　　　　　　　　　　　　　　　　　　　　　　　　　　　　　　　　　The back side of the bar "De Pastorie."

バーエントランス側から「De Pastorie」をみる　　　　　　　　　　バー「De Pastorie」のファサード
The bar "De Pastorie" viewed from the entrance side.　　　　　　The facade of the bar "De Pastorie."

67

サス ロイヤル ホテル アムステルダム

SAS インターナショナル ホテルズがオペレートしているホテルは現在24ケ所あり そのうち 最も新しいのがこのホテルである。アムステルダムの中心 オールドタウンRuslandに位置する関係上 ホテル所有の60%は建造記念物に指定されている。ホテルはレセプションのある新しい北棟(North Wing)と 築後200年以上の古い南棟(South Wing)からなり 両方の建物は地下の広いギャラリーで連結されている。アムステルダムで最初にアトリウム形式をとりいれたこのホテルは オープン ロビーが中央にあり その背後は一段と高く 日本式庭園になっている。ロビー フロアには レストラン「Laxenoxen」と デンマーク風オープン サンドイッチの「Palmboom」 ホテル バー「De Pastorie」がある。これらは古い建物を そのままアトリウムに残したものである。南棟は"アムステルダムの紋章(Wapen van Amsterdam=Coat of arms of Amsterdam)"と呼ばれる古い建物で 62室の部屋 ロイヤル クラブ フィットネス センター 会議室などがある。このホテルはヨーロッパで最新の防火警報システムを備えている。

開業/1990年3月(グランド オープン同年9月) 客室数/247室(北棟:185室 南棟:62室-内 ロイヤルクラブ 32室) 主な施設/ヘルス クラブ(サウナ ソラリウム)

SAS ROYAL HOTEL AMSTERDAM

At present, 24 hotels are operated by SAS International Hotels, including the latest "SAS Royal Hotel Amsterdam." Since it is situated in the old town Rusland, 60% of the properties owned by the hotel are designated as monuments. The hotel is composed of the new North Wing with a reception and the old South Wing built more than 200 years ago – both buildings are linked through a spacious underground gallery. The hotel, which has employed an atrium style for the first time in Amsterdam, has an open lobby in the center, and behind that is a Japanese garden at a higher level. On the lobby floor there is the restaurant "Laxenoxen," the Danish open sandwich shop "Palmboom" and the hotel bar "De Pastorie." They use old buildings which are retained in the atrium. The South Wing is an old building called "Wapen van Amsterdam = Coat of Arms of Amsterdam," having 62 rooms, royal club, fitness center, conference rooms, etc. The hotel itself is equipped with Europe's latest fire protection/alarm system.

Opened/March 1990 (grand opening in September 1990); Number of rooms/247 (North Wing: 185, South Wing: 62 – including 32 royal club rooms); Main facilities/health club (sauna, solarium).

ミーティングルーム The meeting room.

バンケットルーム The banquet room.

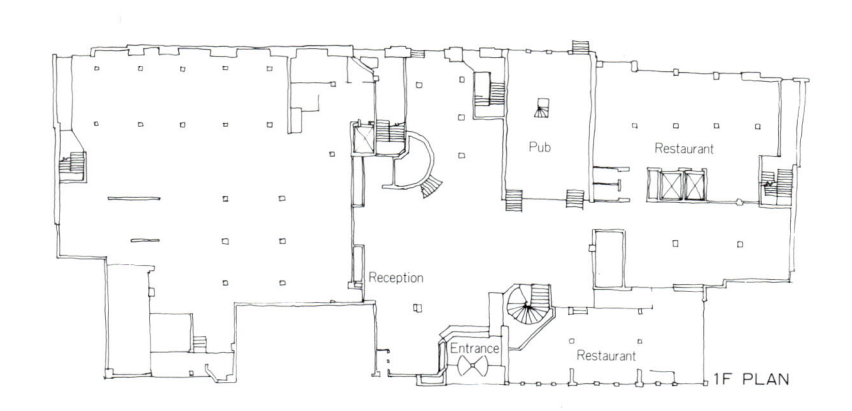

1F PLAN

上・左下・右下/オリエンタル スイート ルーム
Top・left, bottom・right, bottom / The oriental suite room.

エントランス
The entrance.

噴水を通して裏側の外観をみる
The back side appearance viewed across the fountain.

外観全景
The entire view of the appearance.

MARITIM
Hotel
Bonn

Add : Wolvengracht 47, B-1000 Brussels, Belgium
Phone : 2-2192828

マリティーム ホテル ボン

1969年 バルト海沿岸を中心に展開をはじめたMaritim系ホテルは 現在28ケ所 ベッド数約12,000のドイツが誇るリゾート コンベンション チェーンに成長した。"ビジネスの効率"を一貫したフィソロフィー(モットー)としてきたことが その発展の理由かも知れない。この「Maritim Hotel Bonn」は 政府関係の機関が多い官庁街 ゴーデスバーガー アレー(Godesberger Allee)にあり 国際都市ボンにふさわしい コンベンションを主体にした高級ホテルである。中央のエントランスを入ると左側がレセプション 右側はコンベンションエリアで長いロビーが続いている。西側の端には最大1500人収容可能の大ホール「マリティーム(Maritim)」もある。中央の左右二基ずつ設けられたシースルーのエレベーターの利用は キーカードが必要で セキュリティ システムも充実している。

客室数/412室 主な施設/ホール 4室 会議場 11室(最大 3000人の会議可能) プール 地下駐車場

MARITIM HOTEL BONN

The "Maritim Hotel" chain began to develop in 1969 along the coast of the Baltic Sea, and has grown into a resort convention chain operating 28 hotels having about 12,000 beds. The steady development may be due to the consistent pursuit of "business efficiency" as its philosophy (motto).
Situated on Godesberger Allee, a government office quarter with many governmental institutions, the "Maritim Hotel Bonn" is a high-class hotel whose functions are mainly intended for holding conventions — quite becoming to the international city Bonn. From the front entrance one finds a reception on the left side and a convention area on the right side, as well as a long lobby. On the western end there also is a large hall the "Maritim" accommodating up to 1,500 persons. Two each see-through elevators are available on the right and left sides, but they can be used only with a security system.

Number of rooms/412; Main facilities/ 4 halls, 11 conference rooms (capable of holding a conference of up to 3,000 persons), pool, parking lot.

左上/エレベーターを見上げる
左下/廊下を通してコングレス ルームをみる

Left, top / Looking up at the elevator.
Left, bottom / The congress room viewed across the corridor.

ラウンジを通してレセプションをみる

The reception viewed across the lounge.

ロビー

The lobby.

コングレス ルームへの階段　　　　　　　　　　　　　　　　　　　　　　　　　The staircase leading to the congress room.

上/ラウンジ　　　　　　Top / The lounge.
下/ホテル内のショップ　Bottom / The shop in the hotel.

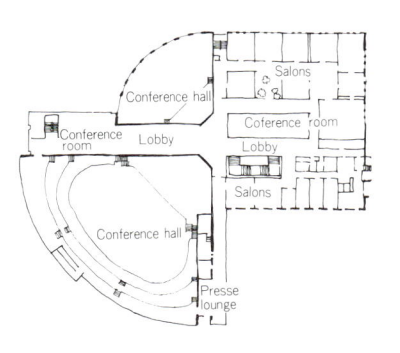

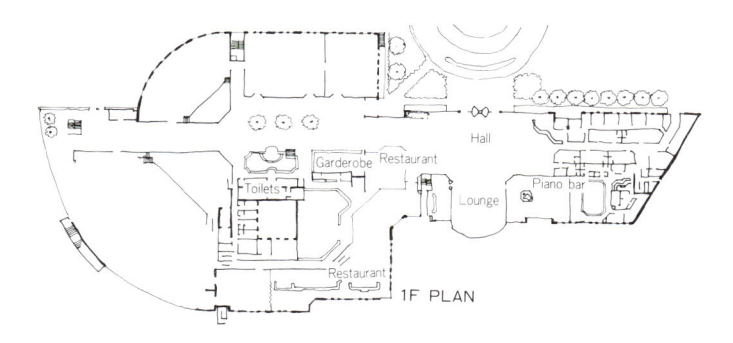

1F PLAN

ピアノ バー / The piano bar.

レストラン「Rôtisserie」 / The restaurant "Rôtisserie."

ブレックファーストとランチのビュッフェ 　　　　　　　　　　　　　　　　　　　　　The breakfast & lunch buffet.

レストラン「La Marée」　　　　　　　　　　　　　　　　　　　　　　　　　　　The restaurant "La Marée."

ファサード
The facade.

ホテル前の回廊
The corridor in front of the hotel.

外観全景
The entire view of the appearance.

HOTEL INTER·CONTINENTAL STUTTGART

Add : Neckarstrasse 60, 70000 Stuttgart, Germany
Phone : 0711-2020-0

ロビー　　　　　　　　　　　　　　　　　　　　　　　　　　The lobby.

メイン エントランス　　The main entrance.

ロビーからレセプションをみる
The reception viewed from the lobby.

ロビーからメイン エントランスを見返す
The main entrance looked back at from the lobby.

レセプション
The reception.

ホテル インター・コンティネンタル
シュトゥットガルト

南部ドイツの工業都市 メルセデス ベンツ (Mercedes Benz)で有名な シュトゥットガルトの中心部 中央駅から東寄りの公園 (Castle Gardens)とネッカーストラッセ (Neckarstrasse)に面して建つこのホテルは 交通の頻繁な通りを避け 公園内のプラネタリウム脇からブリッジをかけて 正面エントランス側にアプローチしている。入口正面のレセプションは ドイツでは珍しく 照明はハロゲンランプのスポットだけである。スイート36室を含む 277部屋の客室 3つのレストラン カクテルラウンジ プールを含む80m²のフィットネスセンター 12の会議場を持つ最大500人の会議が受け入れ可能な規模をもつ 市で最大のコンベンションホテルとなっている。またLufthansa航空のリザベーション オフィスがホテル内にあり 便利である。

開業/1988年9月 客室数/277室(内 スイート36室) 主な施設/宴会 会議場 12室(最大500人収容可能) フィットネスセンター(80m²)

HOTEL INTER · CONTINENTAL STUTTGART

The hotel faces Castle Gardens and Neckarstrasse east of the central station of Stuttgart, an industrial city in southern Germany, which is famous for the Mercedes Benz. Avoiding a street under heavy traffic, it is designed so that guests approach the front entrance across a bridge from beside the planetarium in the park. The reception just behind the entrance is spotlighted only with halogen lamps – very exceptional in Germany. It is the largest convention hotel in the city, having 277 rooms including 36 suite rooms, 3 restaurants, a cocktail lounge, a 80 m² fitness center with a pool, and 12 conference rooms capable of accepting up to 500 persons. A Lufthansa reservation office is conveniently open within the hotel.

Opened/September 1988; Number of rooms/277 (including suite 36); Main facilities/banquet hall, conference hall 12 (accommodating up to 500 persons), fitness center (80 m²)

フィットネス センターのプール　The pool in the fitness center.

バンケット ルーム　The banquet room.

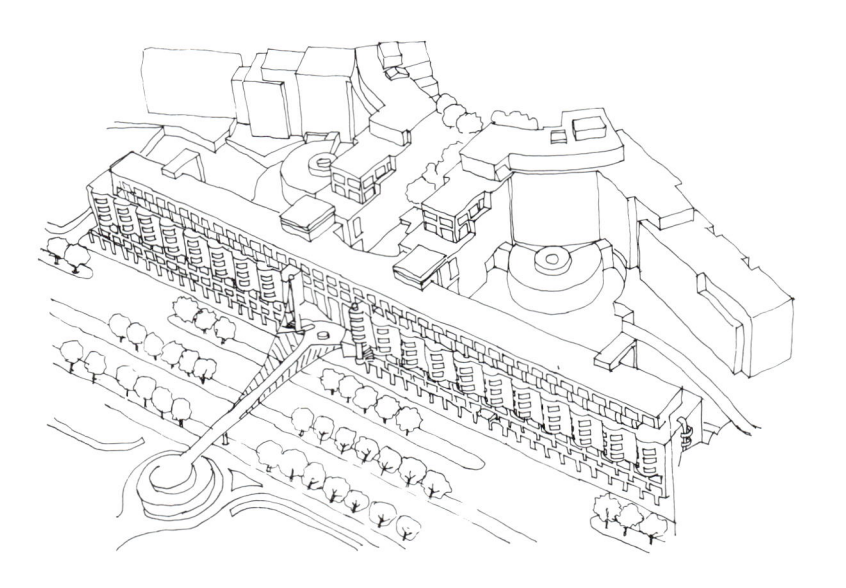

ドイツ クイジーヌ レストラン　　　　　　　　　　　　　　　　　　　　　　　　　　　　　　　　German cuisine restaurant.

レストランのビュッフェ　　　　　　　　　　　　　　　　　　　　　　　　　　　　　　　　　　　The restaurant's buffet.

プレジデント スイートのリビング ルーム　　The living room in the president suite.

ミーティング ルーム　　The meeting room.

バスルーム　　The bathroom.

洗面台のディテール　　The washstand in details.

リビング ルーム

The living room.

ベッド ルーム

The bedroom.

テラス

The terrace.

船上からみるホテル全景

The entire hotel viewed from the deck.

エントランスから吹抜けのロビー方向をみる
The lobby area in the stairwell viewed from the entrance.

廊下のリラックス スペース
The relaxation space along the corridor.

SILJA HOTEL *Ariadne*

Add : Södra Kajen 37, 10052 Stockholm, Sweden
Phone : 08-6657800

2番目のブリッジから吹抜けを俯瞰する   The stairwell overlooked from the 2nd bridge.

吹抜けを俯瞰する

Overlooking the stairwell.

レセプション　　　　　　　　　　　　　　　　　The reception.

"スカイ クラス"のコンシェルジュ　　　　　　　A concierge of "Sky-Class."

ロビーのソファー　　　　　　　　　　　　　　　A sofa on the lobby.

ホテル アリアードン

ストックホルムとヘルシンキの間を結ぶ大型客船 カー フェリーの発着する埠頭にオープンしたホテル。二つの17階建のタワービルが主体で ビル間をガラス階段でジョイントさせたようなスタイルのオフィスビルで 中心部はアトリウムになっている。白く明るいロビーが主役といった感じのホテルである。カウンター ロビー バー ラウンジなどで構成され 落ち着いた雰囲気で レストランは スカンジナビアらしいインテリアで 魚料理が特に美味しい。中央はステップ ダウンして 正面入口に続いている。最上階には イタリアをイメージしたグリーン ブルー グレーを基調にした「スカイ バー(Sky Bar)」があり ここからのストックホルムの島々と湾の眺めは素晴らしい。また この階にはパノラマ状のボード ルームがあり 濃紺の絨毯が敷かれ 静かで設備も充実していて ストックホルムで最も美しい会議場といわれている。

客室数/256室(内 禁煙室 128室 ハンディキャップ専用 4 室 他に13～16階にSky-class ジュニア スイート Lady Business-class ジュニア スイートなどあり) 主な施設/会議場 サウナ マッサージ

HOTEL ARIADNE

The hotel opened on a quay where large liners and car ferries connecting Stockholm and Helsinki dock. It is an office building mainly consisting of two 17-story tower buildings which seem to be connected through a glass staircase, with an atrium in the center. The bright white lobby seems to be playing the main part. The interior is composed of a counter, lobby bar, lounge, etc. in a composed atmosphere, and fish dishes served at the restaurant featuring a Scandinavian interior are especially delicious. The center is stepped down leading to the front entrance. On the highest floor there is the "Sky Bar" whose interior mirrors Italy with green, blue and grey tones, and from the window one can command a wonderful view of islands and the bay of Stockholm. On the same floor there is a panoramic boardroom whose floor is covered with dark blue carpet with a composed atmosphere. Fully equipped with a variety of devices, the boardroom is said to be most beautiful in Stockholm.

Number of rooms/256 (including 128 "no smoking" rooms, 4 rooms for the handicapped, sky-class junior suites, lady business-class junior suites, etc. on the 13 to 16th floors); Main facilities/conference rooms, sauna, massage).

17階にある「スカイ バー」 白夜の時は素晴らしい
"Sky Bar" on the 17th floor; its atmosphere is wonderful at a night with a midnight sun.

同じく17階にある「スカイ コンファレンス」 "Sky Conference" on the 17th floor.

レストラン「Mistral」 　　　　　　　　　　　　　　　　　　　The restaurant "Mistral."

「Mistral」のテーブル廻り　　A table in "Mistral."

「Mistral」のテーブル セッティング
Table setting in "Mistral."

スイート ルーム　リビングからベッド ルームをみる　　The bedroom viewed from the suite's living room.

ベッド ルーム　　The bedroom.

エントランス　ロビーからレセプションをみる　　　　　　　　　　　　　　　　The reception viewed from the entrance lobby.

ポーター　　　　　　　A porter.　　　　　　　レセプション　　　　　　　The reception.

RESO·HOTELS
SERGEL PLAZA

Add : Brunkebergstorg 9, Box 16411, 10327 Stockholm, Sweden
Phone : 08-226600

ロビー デザイン/Alberto Pinto
The lobby design; by Alberto Pinto.

ロビーを通してレセプション方向をみる　The reception area viewed across the lobby.

ロビーに置かれた彫刻
A piece of sculpture placed on the lobby.

ロビー バー　The lobby bar.

レストラン「Anna Rella」のプライベート ディナー ルーム
A private dinner room of the restaurant "Anna Rella."

セルゲル プラザ ホテル
この「Sergel Plaza Hotel」はスウェーデンを中心に ノルウェイ ソ連などで ファーストクラス ホテルを経営するレーソ ホテル(Reso Hotels)チェーンの最高級ホテルの一つである。ストックホルムの中心セルゲル(Sergel)広場にある。以前はスウェーデンの国会議事堂として使用され 現在では ストックホルム市の文化会館になっている建物と同じ棟にある。スウェーデンで最も美しいといわれるホテルのロビーは建築家 アルベルト パント(Albert Pinto)が設計したもので 4ケ所が円形の吹き抜けとなっていて明るい。ブルーと赤い絨毯が鮮やかで 左右のロビー バー(ピアノ バー)とレセプションを含めて スカンジナビア的落ち着きと豪華さを感じさせている。メイン レストランは国際的にも有名な「アンナ レラ(Anna Rella)」。18世紀のクラシカルなスタイルのレストランだが 対照的に使用されている家具類はモダンで 「ベルマン(Bellman)」と「セルジェル(Sergel)」と二つのプライベート用のダイニングも設けられている。

客室数/406室(スイート 12室 ツイン 359室 シングル 35室) 主な施設/宴会 会議場(最大会議 150人 バンケット 200人 パーティ 400人収容可能) 総合ビューティ センター(エステティック ボディケア) サウナ マッサージ ソラリウム

SERGEL PLAZA HOTEL

"Sergel Plaza Hotel" is one of the first class hotels in the Reso Hotels chain which operates first class hotels mainly in Sweden, as well as in Norway, the U.S.S.R., etc. It is situated on the Sergel Plaza which is in the center of Stockholm. It is in the same building which was formerly used as the Capitol or Seat of Government of Sweden and is currently used as a culture hall by Stockholm City. The hotel's lobby which is said to be most the beautiful in Sweden, was designed by architect Albert Pinto, and it is very bright with four stairwells. The floor is covered with a vivid blue & red carpet, and with lobbies on the right and left sides, bar (piano bar), and reception, the interior generally imports a composed Scandinavian atmosphere and is gorgeous. The main restaurant is "Anna rella" which is internationally known. It is a classical restaurant of the 18th century, but contrastingly enough the furniture is modern; two private dining rooms the "Bellman" and "Sergel" are also installed.

Number of rooms/406 (12 suites, 359 twin and 35 single); Main facilities/banquet and conference rooms (max. capacity is 150 persons for conference space, 200 persons for banquet space and 400 for party space, general beauty center (aesthetic body care), sauna, massage, solarium.

レストラン「Anna Rella」

The restaurant "Anna Rella."

「コルビジェ スイート（Le Corbusier Suite）」 "Le Corbusier Suite."

「ウィンザー スイート（The Windsor Suite）」
"The Windsor Suite."

ツインのベッド ルーム
A twin bedroom.

ファサード　　　　　　　　　　　　　　　　　　　　　　　　　　　　　　　　　The facade.

SCANDIC CROWN HOTEL

Add　：Kanalvägen 10, 19461 Upplands Väsby, Sweden
Phone : 0760-95510

スカンディック クラウン ホテル

このホテルは ストックフォルムと アルランダ(Arlanda)空港の中間点にある GLG企業センター内に1991年7月にオープンした。設計はReneé Pfenniger。延べ300,000㎡の広さのこのセンターには インターナショナル マルチ企業140社がテナントとして入っている。
「Scandic Crown Hotel」は ヨーロッパでは初めてのエコロジー トロピカル ガーデンを持つホテルで 1,300㎡のガーデンには フロリダから直送した12mほどのシュロなど約2,500本の熱帯植物が植えられている。その周囲のグランド フロアには 320人が収容できるボールルームがある。ロビーの左側のエスカレーターで上がった位置から トロピカル ガーデンの上へブリッジがかけられ このレベルの周囲には 20ケ所に会議場が設けられている。10階には 8×4mのプール付きのフィットネス センターがあり サウナ ジム ソラリウムなどを完備し マッサージ サービスもある。ホテルの廊下のパネルには蛍光塗料が塗られ 緊急時の非難誘導は完璧で 安全性の高いホテルとして注目されている。

開業/1991年7月 客室数/236室(スイート 8室 ダブル 128室 ビジネス ルーム 100室)
主な施設/会議場(24室) トロピカル ガーデン (1,300㎡ー室内ではヨーロッパ最大規模) フィットネス センター(8×4mプール ジム サウナ ソラリウム マッサージ)

SCANDIC CROWN HOTEL

The hotel opened in July 1991 within the GLG Corporate Center which lies on the midpoint between Stockholm and the Arlanda Airport. Designed by Reneé Pfenniger, the center houses 140 multi-national enterprises within a total of a 300 000 m² space. The "Scandic Crown Hotel" has Europe's first ecological tropical garden, and on a 1,300 m² garden about 2,500 tropical plants are grown, including hemp palms about 12 m high which were directly brought in from Florida. On the surrounding grand floor there is a ballroom capable of accommodating 320 persons. There is a bridge crossed from above the left side of the lobby reached by an elevator, to a level above the tropical garden, and around the area there are 20 conference rooms. On the 10th floor there is a fitness center with a 8×4m pool, and it is also fully equipped with a sauna, gymnasium, solarium, etc.; massage service is also available. The panels on the hotel's passages are coated with fluorescent paint, and evacuation guidance in an emergency is perfect. Thus, the hotel is drawing attention as a very safe hotel.

Opened/July 1991; Number of rooms/236 (suite 8, double 128, business room 100); Main facilities/conference rooms (24), tropical garden (1,300 m² — one of the largest indoor gardens in Europe), fitness center (8×4 m pool, gym., sauna, solarium, massage).

コンファレンス ロビーから客室棟を見上げる
The guest room building overlooked from the conference lobby.

エントランス
The entrance.

右/このホテルのシンボルであるライオンの彫刻
Right/ The lion's sculpture which is a symbol of the hotel.

外観全景　　　　　　　　　　　　　　　　　　　　　　　　　　　The entire appearance.

レセプション　　　　　The reception.

スイミング プール　　　　The swimming pool.

コンファレンスのレセプション
The reception for the conference space.

ホテル自慢のセキュリティーシステム　停電になるとパネルが自動的に光る（螢光色）
The security system – the pride of the hotel; the panel glows (emitting fluorescent light) when a power failure occurs.

ストックホルムで最もエキゾチックなガーデン　　　　　　　　　　　　　　　　　　　The most exotic garden in Stockholm.

ガーデン内の樹木にミスト(mist＝霧)を吹くのが一日の始まり　　　　A day starts with spraying a mist over trees in the garden.

ガーデン内のレストラン　　The restaurant in the garden.

ガーデン内のパブ カウンター　A pub counter in the garden.

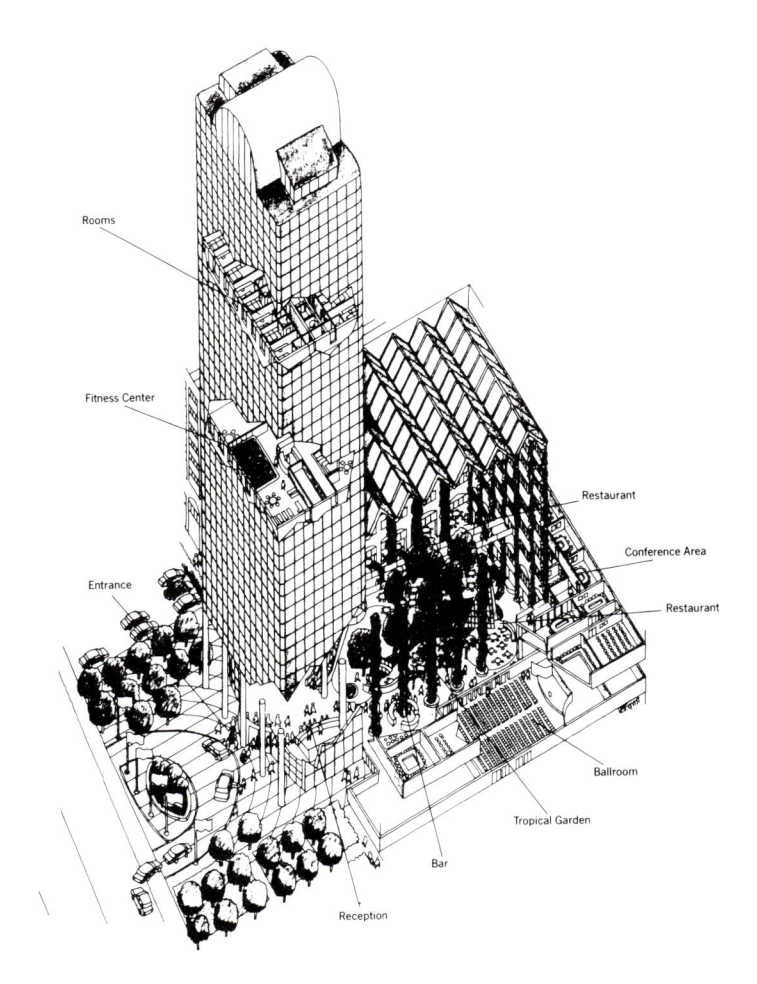

Rooms
Fitness Center
Entrance
Restaurant
Conference Area
Restaurant
Ballroom
Tropical Garden
Bar
Reception

99

スイートのリビング ルーム　　　　　　　　　　　　　　　　　　　　The suite's living room.

ガーデンに面したリビング ルーム　　The living room facing the garden.

スイートのベッド ルーム　　　　　The suite's bedroom.

西側外観をみる　左後方に見えるのはターミナルからの入口
The western appearance; the entrance from the terminal is visible on the rear left side.

エントランス前に立つポーター
A porter standing before the entrance.

外観全景
The entire appearance.

STERLING HOTEL

Add   : Terminal 4, Heathrow Airport, Hounslow Middlesex, U.K.
Phone : 081-7597755

モーターロードを通して外観をみる
The appearance viewed across the motor road.

101

高い空間に彫刻を配したラウンジ　　　　　　　　　　　　　The lounge with pieces of sculpture placed in a high space.

ラウンジを俯瞰する　　　　　　　　　　　　　　　　　　　　　　Overlooking the lounge.

エントランス　　　　　The entrance.

エレベーター ブリッジ　　　　　The elevator bridge.

エレベーターは後ろから外光を受けると光る
The elevator glistens when receiving external light from the rear.

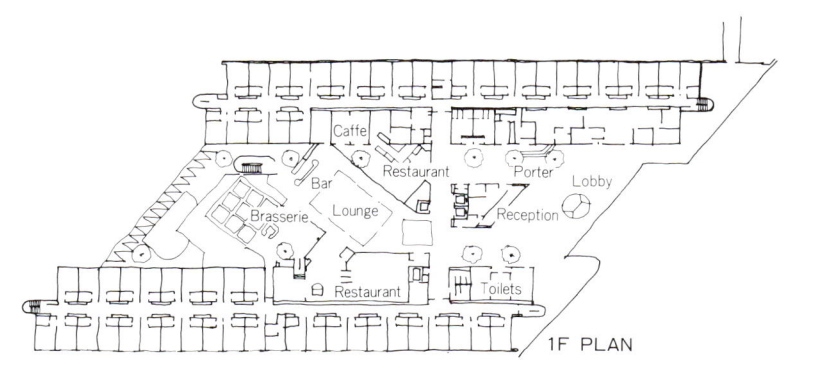

1F PLAN

103

ラウンジ中央のリラックス コーナー
The relaxation corner in the center of the lounge.

レセプション
The reception.

レセプションからエントランス方向をみる
The entrance area viewed from the reception.

ヒースロー スターリング ホテル

ロンドン ヒースロー(Heathrow)空港のターミナル4に ガトウィック(Gatwick)空港の北ターミナルに次いで 二番目の「Sterling Hotel」が1990年11月にオープンした。英国航空の出資によるBAA Hotels Ltd経営のこのホテルは 5層にわたるガラスウォールの横に長い菱形のアトリウム建築で レセプション バー カフェ 2ケ所のレストラン ヘア サロン ギフト ショップ 英国航空チェックイン カウンター そしてエレベーターなどを内包する 大きなオープン空間を持っている。英国空港が発着するターミナル4と メトロ駅からホテルまでは アルミニュームのリンクで結ばれている。各部屋には"Thorn Dataview"と呼ぶリモート コントロールのコンピューター インフォメーション システムが設置され 居ながらしてエアラインやホテルのインフォメーション チェック アウトなどのサービスが得られる。設計は建築がManser Associates インテリアはPeter Glyn Smith Associates。
開業/1990年11月 客室数/400ベッド(内 ジュニア スイート 4室 スターリングClub 82室)各部屋にコンピューター インフォメーション システム設置 主な施設/会議場(最大300人まで収容可能) スパ ヘルス クラブ(ジム サウナ プール)

レストラン　The restaurant.

バー　The bar.

カフェ　The cafe.

HEATHROW STERLING HOTEL

The "Heathrow Sterling Hotel" is the 2nd "Sterling Hotel" opened in November 1990 at Terminal 4 of Heathrow Airport, London, next only to the 1st hotel that opened at the North Terminal of Gatwick Airport. Financed by British Airlines and operated by BAA Hotels Ltd., the hotel features a long rhombic atrium installed beside a 5-layer glass wall, and it has a large open space accommodating a reception, bar, cafe, two restaurants, a hair salon, gift shop. British Airlines checkin counter, elevators, etc. The Terminal 4, metro station and hotel are connected through aluminum links. Each room is equipped with a remotely controlled computer information system called "Thorn Dataview" so that, while staying in the room, guests can receive airline or hotel information, checkout details, etc. The architecture was designed by Manser Associates, while the interior was designed by Glyn Smith Associates.

Opened/November 1990; Number of rooms/ 400 (including 4 junior suite rooms, 82 Sterling Club rooms), each room is equipped with a computer information system; Main facilities/conference space (capable of accommodating up to 300 persons), spa health club (gym., sauna, pool).

プール サイド / The poolside.

プールへのアプローチ / An approach to the pool.

プールに下りる階段から外をみる / An outside view from the staircase leading down to the pool.

スイートのリビング ルーム   The suite's living room.

シングル ルーム   A single room.   バス ルーム   A bathroom.

ファサード
The facade.

Hotel Sofitel
TOULOUSE CENTRE

Add : 84 Allées Jean-Jaurès, 3100 Toulouse, France
Phone : 61-10 23 10

右/外観全景
Right / The entire appearance.

ロビー中央からエントランス方向をみる　　　　　　　　　　　　　The entrance area viewed from the center of the lobby.

エントランス　　　　The entrance.

レセプション　　　　The reception.

ロビー中央をみる

ホテル ソフィテル トゥロウーズ

南フランスの工業都市　ヨーロッパ航空機産業のメッカであり　エアバスの生産地として知られるトゥロウーズ(Toulouse)に「Hotel Sofitel Toulouse」がオープンした。ショッピング街で　駅から徒歩で5分の中心部 Gare Matabiau に立地している。レセプション フロアには　銀色系の大理石をふんだんに使用し　明るくゲストを迎えてくれる。ビジネスマンたちに最大限の"ホーム＆オフィス"を提供することに徹したという客室は　快適でリラックスできる。レセプションの右側には　20世紀初期のデコ(Art Deco)スタイルのレストランがある。左側はピアノバー。ハープの演奏なども聞かれ　明るい雰囲気である。レセプションやコンファレンス設備が充実しており　ビジネス客のためのビジネスセンターの役割をはたしている。

客室数/119室(内 スイート 14室)　主な施設/宴会　会議場(最大 200人収容)

HOTEL SOFITEL TOULOUSE

The "Hotel Sofitel Toulouse" opened in Toulouse an industrial city in South France, and is known as a mecca of the European aircraft industry and especially for the production of airbuses. It is situated on Gare Matabiau, a shopping street in the center of the city, which is 5 minutes on foot from the station. The reception floor abundantly uses silver marble, thus welcoming guests in a bright atmosphere. The guest rooms have been designed to offer the best possible "home & office" to businessmen so that they can feel comfortable and be relaxed. There is a restaurant on the right side of the reception which features an art déco style from early in the 20th century. There is a piano bar on the left side where guests can enjoy harp performances, etc. in a bright atmosphere. The hotel is fully finished with reception and conference equipment in order to play the role as a business center for business guests.

Number of rooms/119 (including suite 14);　Main facilities/banquet and conference rooms (max. capacity is 200 persons).

メザニンからロビーを俯瞰する
Overlooking the lobby from the mezzanine.

The center of the lobby.　メザニン　The mezzanine.

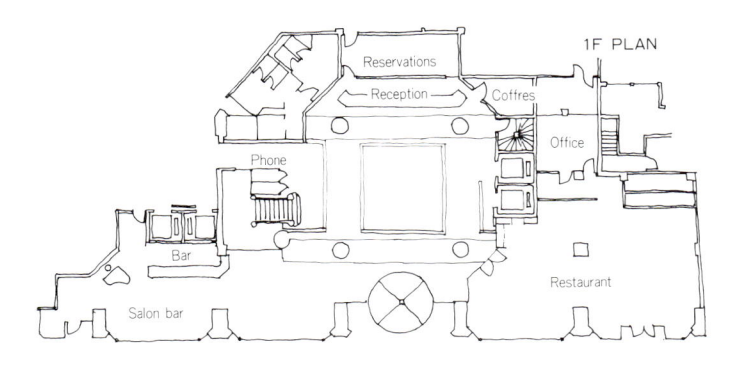

1F PLAN

ロビーからメザニンに上がる階段
The staircase leading from the lobby up to the mezzanine.

レストラン

The restaurant.

サロン バー

The salon bar.

スイートのリビング ルーム

The suite's living room.

スイート ルームに設置されたパソコン
A personal computer installed in the suite room.

スイートのベッド ルーム
The suite's bedroom.

高層部分の外観 　　　　　　　　The appearance of higher floors.

外観全景 　　　The entire appearance.

かつてのスケートの女王　ソニア(Sonia Henje)の像
The statue of Sonja Henie who was once the queen of skating.

メイン エントランス 　　　　　　　　　　The main entrance.

RESO·HOTELS

OSLO PLAZA
Plaza Tower

Add : Sonja Henies pl, 3. N-0107 Oslo, Norway
Phone : 02-171000

114

中央に木彫を配したロビーを俯瞰する   Overlooking the lobby accented with a piece of wood carving in the center.

オスロ プラザ ホテル

北欧一といわれるレーソ (Reso) ホテル系の「Oslo Plaza」は 地上117m 37階建の高層建築で トップからは オスロ市内 ホルメンコーレン (Holmenkollen) のジャンプ台 郊外に続く山々などの眺望が素晴らしい。延床面積は45,000m²で 客室はスタンダード ルームでも26m²とかなりゆったりとした広さである。海抜117mの高さにあるフィットネス センター「アーカーセルヴァ (Akerselva)」で 街を見下ろしながら泳ぐこともできる。最上階にはバーやディスコもある。各フロアに彫刻が置かれているのもスカンジナビア的である。
開業/1990年3月 客室数/685室(内 スイート20室) 主な施設/宴会 会議場(Sonja Henie Ballroom 890m² Munchsalen 168m² など合計2000人収容可能) フィットネス センター

OSLO PLAZA HOTEL

"Oslo Plaza" of the Reso Hotel chain, which is said to be the largest in Scandinavia, is a high-rise (117 m high) building having 37 stories above ground. From the highest floor one can command a wonderful view of Oslo City, the Holmenkollen ski jumping slopes, the mountains extending to the suburbs, etc. The total floor area is 45,000 m², and guest rooms are standard but as spacious as 26 m². At the fitness center "Akerselva" which is 117 m above sea level, one can swim while overlooking the street. There is also a bar and disco on the highest floor. It is also quite Scandinavian in that each floor is accented with sculpture.

Opened/March 1990; Number of rooms/685 (including suite 20); Main facilities/banquet and conference spaces (Sonja Henie Ballroom 890 m², Munchsalen 168 m², etc. capable of accommodating 2,000 persons in total), fitness center.

右上/ロビー バーからレセプション方向をみる
右中/エントランス前からレセプション方向をみる
右下/メイン エントランス廻り

Right, top / The reception area viewed from the lobby bar.
Right, center / The reception area viewed from the entrance.
Right, bottom / The main entrance area.

ボール ルーム　　　　　　　　　　　　　　　　　　　　　　　　　　The ballroom.

地上117mにあるスイミング プール
The swimming room 117 m high above ground.

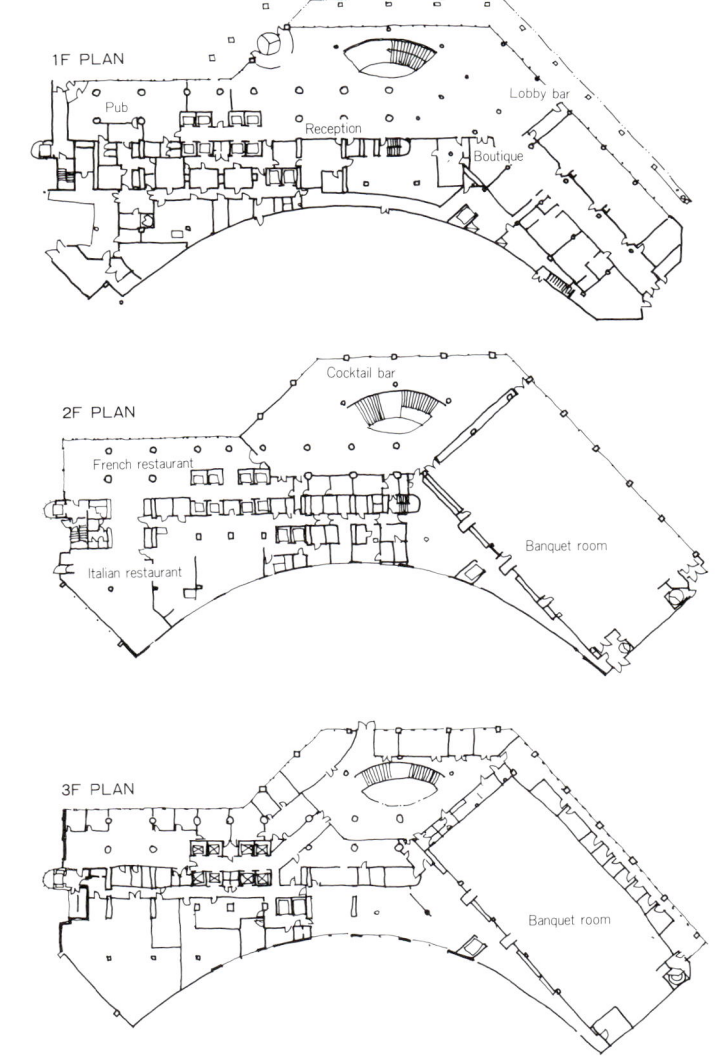

1F PLAN — Pub, Reception, Lobby bar, Boutique

2F PLAN — French restaurant, Italian restaurant, Cocktail bar, Banquet room

3F PLAN — Banquet room

フレンチ ブラッスリー「Brasserie Abelone」 French brasserie "Brasserie Abelone."

ロビー バー The lobby bar.

イタリアン レストラン「Ristorante Lakata」　　　Italian restaurant "Ristorante Lakata."

ダンシング バー「Plaza Sky」　　　The dancing bar "Plaza Sky."

「フレンチ クラシック(French Classic)」のベッド ルーム　　　　The bedroom of "French Classic."

スイート ルームのバー　　The suite room's bar.

スイート ルームのダイニング　　The suite's dining room.

運河を挟んでホテルをみる
The hotel viewed across a canal.

レセプション　フィンランド産の花崗石が使用されている
The reception; finished with the Finnish granite.

ロビー　暖炉には夕方になると火が入れられる
The lobby; the fireplace is lit up in the evening.

HOTEL STRAND INTER·CONTINENTAL

Add : John Stenbergin Ranfa 4, 00530 Helsinki, Finland
Phone : 90-39351

最上階からアトリウムを俯瞰する The atrium overlooked from the highest floor.

アトリウム プラザのレストラン The restaurant of the atrium plaza.

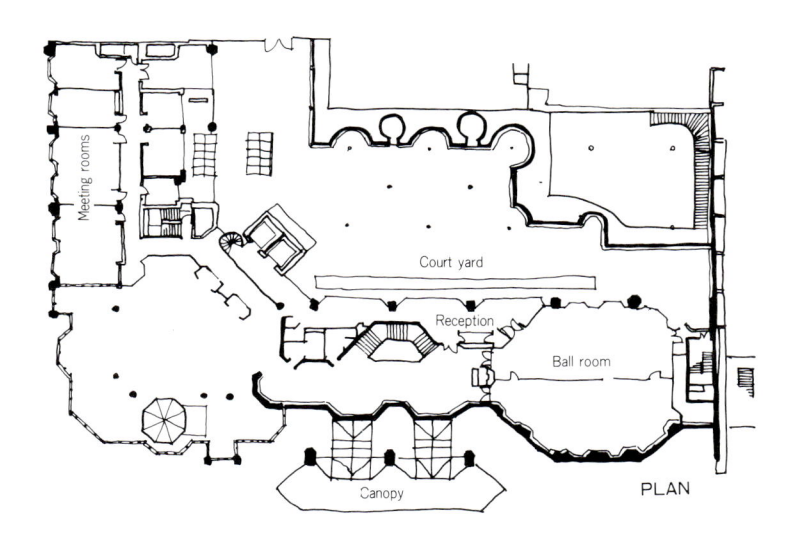

ホテル ストランド インター・コンティネンタル

ヘルシンキの運河のほとりに面して建てられた「Strand Inter・Continental」は バルト海を望む国際的クラスの新しいホテルである。キャノピーのあるエントランスを入った正面のレセプション アトリウム プラザ エレベーター ロビーは 空間の広がりが いかにも北欧的である。素材として使用されている大理石にも見るべきものがある。ロビーとアトリウムの床は花崗石の結晶の大きい"カレリアン ミスティック"や "ドロマイト"が使用されている。ラウンジ バーの手前のロビーには ガス式暖炉があり 夕方には火が入れられ ムードを高める。ホテル内には随所に 環境デザインやガラス セラミックなどのクラフト製品が多く さすがに芸術 デザインの国 フィンランドらしい。

開業/1988年11月 客室数/184室(プレジデント スイート 1室 パノラマ スイート 5室 ジュニア スイート 4室 スタジオ ルーム 16室 ダブル 22室 ツイン ダブル 131室 キング ルーム 5室) 主な施設/宴会 会議場(ボールルーム 220㎡ 200人収容) キャビネット ルーム(合計 180㎡) フィンランド サウナクラブ(予約制)

HOTEL STRAND INTER · CONTINENTAL

The "Strand Inter · Continental" was constructed facing a canal in Helsinki and is a new international hotel commanding a view of the Baltic Sea. The front reception behind the canopied entrance, atrium plaza, and elevator lobby are quite spacious and Scandinavian. The marble used as a material is also noteworthy. The lobby and atrium are floored with "Kalelian Mystique," "Dromite," etc. which feature large granite crystals. The lobby in front of the lounge bar has a gas-fired fireplace which is lit in the evening to enliven the mood. Here and there the hotel is accented with pieces of craft work, including environmental designs, glass and ceramic ware, reminding us of the fact that Finland is a country of art and design.

Opened/November 1988; Number of rooms/president suite 1, panorama suite 5, junior suite 4, studio room 16, double 22, twin double 131, king room 5); Main facilities/banquet and conference spaces (ballroom 220 m² – capable of accommodating up to 200 persons), cabinet room (total space 180 m²), Finland sauna club (reservation system).

上・下/アトリウム プラザにある環境アート
Top · bottom / The environmental art at the atrium plaza.

グルメ レストラン「Pamir」

The gourmet restaurant "Pamir."

「Pamir」のテーブル セッティング

Table setting at "Pamir."

「Pamir」窓際のガラス器アート

Pieces of glassware art on the window side of "Pamir."

ボール ルーム
The ballroom.

8階にあるサウナ クラブのプール　天井には木が多く使用されている
The pool of the sauna club on the 8th floor; the ceiling uses a lot of wood.

パノラマ スイートのダイニング ルーム

The panorama suite's dining room.

ジュニア スイートのダイニング ルーム
The junior suite's dining room.

ジュニア スイートのベッド ルーム
The junior suite's bedroom.

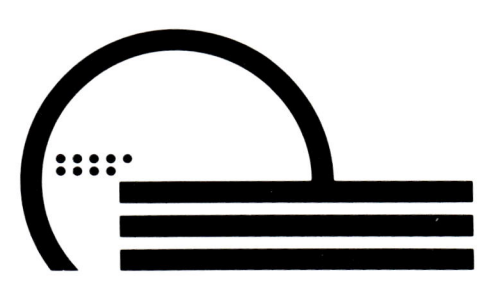

STOCKHOLM GLOBE HOTEL

Add : Box 10004, 12126 Stockholm-Globen, Sweden
Phone : 08-7259000

ストックホルム グローブ ホテル
ストックホルムでの 第二次世界大戦後最大の建築プロジェクトの一つ Globen City が完成した。この一大コンプレックスは メインであるアリーナとショッピング センター そしてホテルで構成され ストックホルム市の中心部から 僅か数キロ南側に位置している。コンサート 各種室内競技 展示会など 多目的に利用される球形のアリーナは スカンジナビアはもちろん 世界でも珍しいコンベンション シティーで 新しいストックホルムのシンボルにふさわしい建築で 収容数は16,000人である。「Stockholm Globe Hotel」はアリーナの南側にあり 会議場を主目的に建設されたものである。7階の「レストランArena」からは アイスホッケーやコンサートなど アリーナでのイベントを見ながら また 各テーブルの背後のTVモニターの実況を見ながら食事ができる。
客室数/290室 主な施設/宴会 会議場(13室) オーディオ ルーム(220席)

STOCKHOLM GLOBE HOTEL

The construction of "Globen City," which was one of the largest architectural projects in Stockholm after the Second World War, has completed. The large complex is composed of an arena (in the main), shopping center and hotel, and is situated only a few km south of the center of Stockholm City. The multi-purpose arena is designed so that it can be used for concerts, various types of indoor sports, exhibitions, etc. Thus, it serves as a convention center quite rare not merely Scandinavia but also in the world, and is quite suitable as a new symbol of Stockholm. It can accommodate 16,000 persons. The "Stockholm Globe Hotel" south of the arena was constructed primarily to serve as a conference space. From the "Restaurant Arena" on the 7th floor one can view ice hockey, concerts or any other event in the area, and view a play-by-play broadcast on the TV monitor behind each table while eating.

Number of rooms/290; Main facilities/banquet and conference spaces (13 rooms), audio room (220 seats).

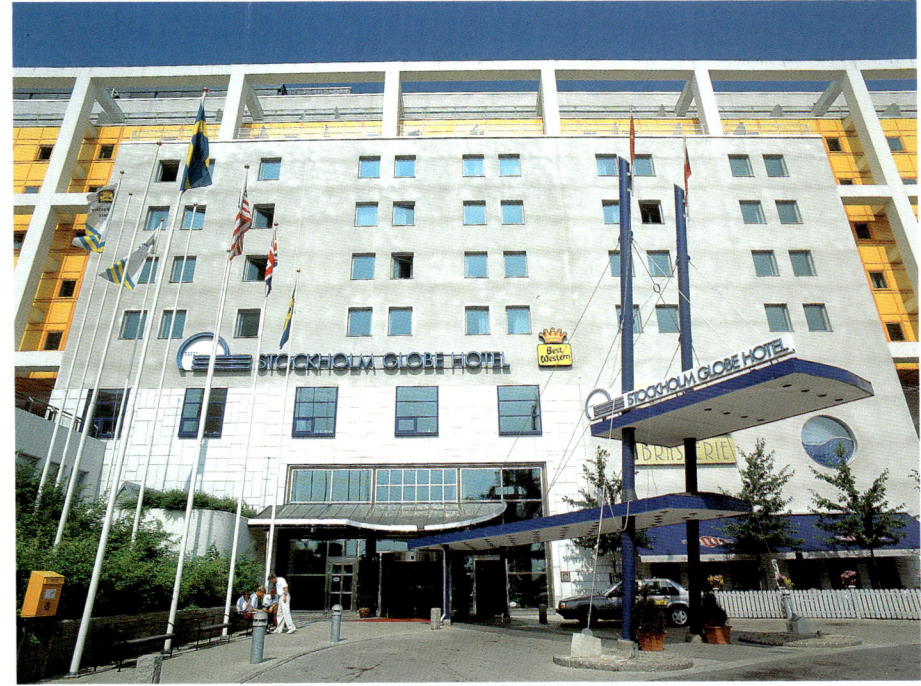

上/外観 バックの円形の建物がグローブ アリーナ
下/ファサード
Top / The appearance; the round building at the back is "Globe Arena."
Bottom / The facade.

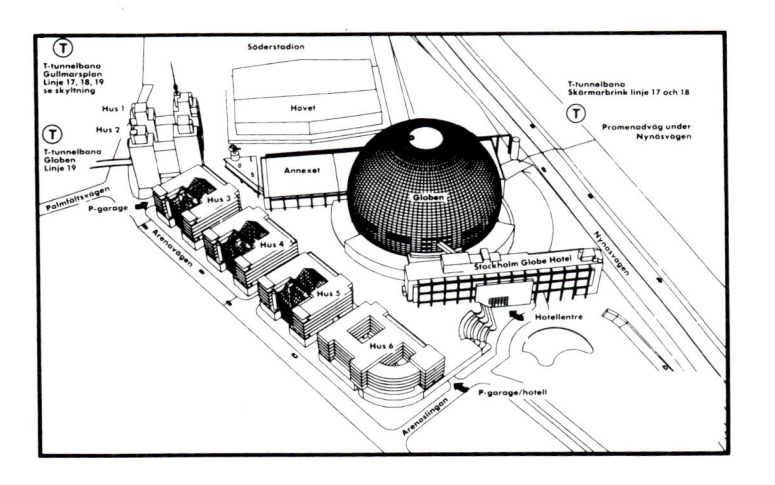

コンファレンス フロア（2階）からロビーを俯瞰する

コンファレンス フロアのロビー
The lobby on the conference floor.

ロビーからコンファレンス フロアを見上げる
Looking up at the conference floor from the lobby.

レセプション
The reception.

The lobby overlooked from the conference floor (2nd floor).

「レストラン Arena」 ゲーム コンサートなどを見ながら食事ができる　　"Restaurant Arena"; guests can enjoy eating while viewing a game, concert, etc.

「レストラン Arena」のランチ用テーブル セッティング　　Table setting for lunch at "Restaurant Arena."

フレンチ スタイルのバー「Tabac」　　　　　　　　　　　　　　　　　　　　　　　　　　French style bar "Tabac."

「レストラン Arena」からバー「Tabac」のカウンターをみる
The counter of the bar "Tabac" viewed from "Restaurant Arena."

コンファレンスのオーディオ ルーム 　　　　　　　　　　　The audio room on the conference floor.

ベッド ルームを通してリビング ルームをみる 　　　　　　　The living room viewed through the bedroom.

Traditional Hotels／トラディショナル ホテル

HOTEL RITZ BARCELONA《Barcelona, Spain》／ホテル リッツ バルセロナ《スペイン、バルセロナ》
Add : Gran Via Cortes Catalanas 668, 08010 Barcelona, Spain　　Phone : 93-3185200
.... 134

HOTEL NEGRESCO《Nice, France》／ホテル ネグレスコ《フランス、ニース》
Add : 37 Promenade des Anglais, BP 379, 06007 Nice, France　　Phone : 93-88 39 51
.... 142

THE RITZ LONDON《London, U.K.》／ザ リッツ ロンドン《イギリス、ロンドン》
Add : Piccadilly, London W1, U.K.　　Phone : 071-493-8181
.... 150

HOLMENKOLLEN PARK HOTEL《Oslo, Norway》／ホルメンコーレン パーク ホテル《ノルウェイ、オスロ》
Add : Kongeveien 26, N 0390 Oslo 3, Norway　　Phone : 02-146090
.... 156

COPENHAGEN ADMIRAL HOTEL《Copenhagen, Denmark》／コペンハーゲン アドミラル ホテル《デンマーク、コペンハーゲン》
Add : Toldbodgade 24-28, DK-1253 Copenhagen K, Demnark　　Phone : 33-118282
.... 163

BONAPRTE HOTEL《Milano, Italy》／ボナパルト ホテル《イタリー、ミラノ》
Add : Via De Amicis 32, 20123 Milano, Italy　　Phone : 2-72000581
.... 169

HÔTEL PLAZA ATHÉNÉE《Paris, France》／オテル プラザ アテネ《フランス、パリ》
Add : 25 Avenue Montaigne 75008 Paris, France　　Phone : 1-47 23 78 33
.... 174

ST.ANDREWS OLD COURSE HOTEL《St.Andrews, U.K.》／セント アンドリュース オールド コース ホテル《イギリス、セント アンドリュース》
Add : St.Andrews, Fife, Scotland, U.K.　　Phone : 0334-74371
.... 180

THE DORCHESTER《London, U.K.》／ザ ドルチェスター《イギリス、ロンドン》
Add : Park Lane London W1, U.K.　　Phone : 071-629-8888
.... 187

GRAND HOTEL STOCKHOLM《Stockholm, Sweden》／グランド ホテル ストックホルム《スウェーデン、ストックホルム》
Add : S.Blasieholmshamnen 8, P.O.Box 16424, S-10327 Stockholm, Sweden　　Phone : 08-221020
.... 193

トップ ライトのあるホールの天井を見上げる

Looking up at the hall's ceiling having a top light.

外観全景　市の中心通り　グラン ビア (Gran Via) に面している
The entire appearance; facing the Gran Via, the central street of the city.

ロビー サイドからホールを通してピアノ ラウンジをみる
The piano lounge viewed from the lobby side through the hall.

Hotel Ritz
Barcelona

Add　: Gran Via Cortes Catalanas 668, 08010 Barcelona, Spain
Phone : 93-3185200

ロビー The lobby.

ロビーからレセプションをみる
The reception viewed from the lobby.

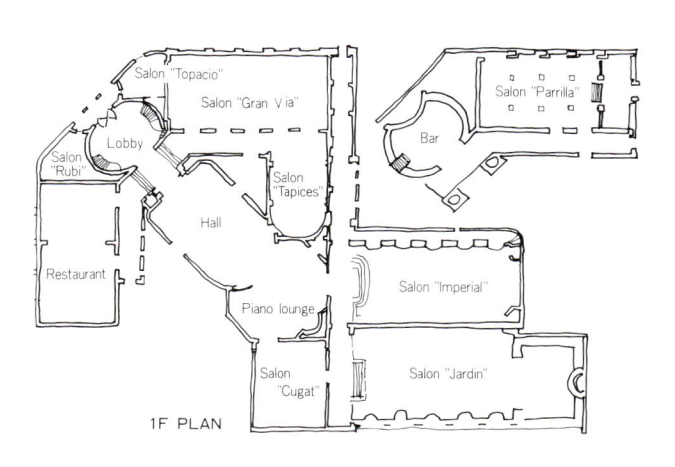

1F PLAN

ピアノ ラウンジ

The piano lounge.

ホテル リッツ バルセロナ

1919年に開業した「Hotel Ritz Barcelona」は 市の中心 街路樹の美しいグランピア(Glan Via)大通りに面して建ち 今日までバルセロナの発展とともに 伝統と気品を重んじてきた。五ツ星デラックスホテルである。1979年に改装され 室内には近代的な設備を備えたモダンなホテルに生まれ変わった。ロビー奥にあるメイン ホールと それに続くステップダウンしたピアノ ラウンジには 天井からの自然光が柔らかくいきわたり ゆったりとしたソファや家具の配置は リッツにふさわしい空間をつくり出している。これまでに多くの政治家 文化人 アーティストなどがゲストとして滞在し この雰囲気をこよなく愛したという。

開業/1979年(改装) 客室数/161室(内 スイート5室 ロイヤル スイート含む)

HOTEL RITZ BARCELONA

Opened in 1919, the "Ritz Hotel Barcelona" stands facing the Gran Via which passes the center of the city with beautiful roadside trees. It is a deluxe 5-star hotel which has been operated to date along with the development of Barcelona, while making much of tradition and dignity. As a result of redecoration in 1979, it has been renewed into a modern hotel furnished with modern interior equipment. Natural light from the ceiling softly comes down on the main hall on an inner part of the lobby and the piano lounge stepping down from the lobby. The spacious layout of sofas, furniture, etc. creates an atmosphere becoming to the Ritz. So far, many politicians, men of culture, artists, etc. have stayed here, specially loving the atmosphere.

Opened/1979 (redecorated); Number of rooms/161 (including 5 usual and royal suite rooms).

ピアノ ラウンジのソファ席　　　　　　　　　　　　　　　　　　　　　　　　　　　　　　　　The sofa seating in the piano lounge.

ピアノ ラウンジ ディナー パーティーのレセプション
The piano lounge; the reception for a dinner party.

ピアノ ラウンジ パーティーのテーブル セッティング
The piano lounge; table setting for a party.

上・下／レストラン「Diana」　　　　　　　　　　　　　　　　　　　Top・bottom / The restaurant "Diana."

上・下／サロン「Imperial」　　　　　　　　　　　　　　　　　　　　　　　　　　Top · bottom / The salon "Imperial."

スイートのリビング ルーム　　　　　　　　　　　　　　　　　　　　　　　　　　　The suite's living room.

スイートのローマ風バス ルーム　　The suite's Roman bathroom. 　　　スイートのバス ルーム　　The suite's bathroom.

スイートのリビング ルーム

The suite's living room.

スイートのベッド ルーム

The suite's bedroom.

ニースの海岸通り　プロムナード　デ　ザングレ(Promenade des Anglais)に面したホテルの外観
The appearance of the hotel facing the Promenade des Anglais – a street along the Coast of Nice.

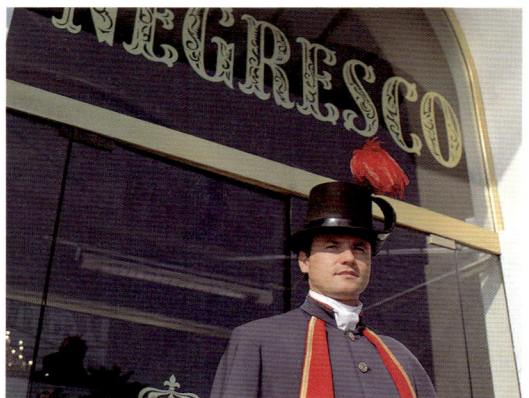

ドアマン　　　　　　　　　　The doorman.

NEGRESCO

Add　：37 Promenade des Anglais, BP 379, 06007 Nice, France
Phone：93-88 39 51

右上/エントランス右側のレセプション
右下/エントランス左側のコンシェルジュ
Right, top / The reception on the right side of the entrance.
Right, bottom / A concierge on the left side of the entrance.

「Salon Royal」中央のシャンデリアは 16,309個のクリスタルで構成されている　床の絨毯は世界一大きい
The chandelier in the center of "Salon Royal" is composed of 16,309 crystals; the floor carpet is largest in the world.

「Salon Royal」のソファとテーブル
The sofa and table in "Salon Royal."

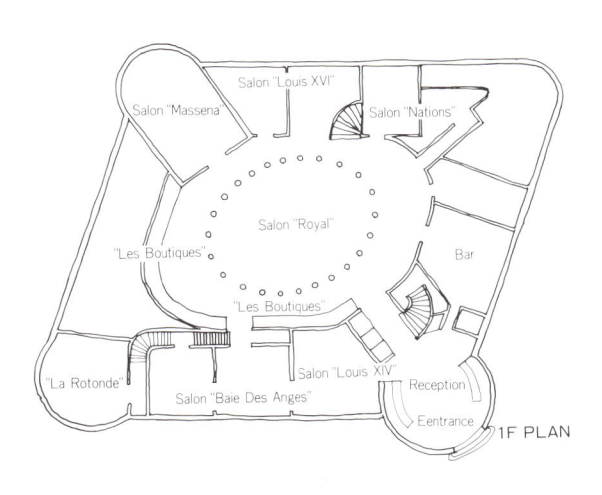

コンファレンス ルーム　　The conference room.

ホテル ネグレスコ

コート ダジュール(Cote d'Azur)最大の都市ニース(Nice)のリゾートや観光客で賑わいをみせるプロムナード デ ザングレに面する「Hotel Negresco」のパレス風のファサードはニースのランド マーク的な存在である。昔からニースには年間を通じてアメリカの富豪 ヨーロッパの皇室 貴族たちが集まってきたが"そうした人たちを迎えるのにふさわしいホテル"をコンセプトに 1913年にルーマニア生まれのアンリ ネグレスコ(Henri Negresco)によって創立されたのが この四ツ星L高級ホテルである。ホテル内の家具 調度品 タペストリーなどは どれもが歴史的で豪華なものであり これまでのオーナーの徹底したコレクション スピリットが感じられる。中央にある「サロン ロワイヤル(Salon Royal)」には ステンド グラスのドームの下に ルイ14世時代の椅子や 円形の2,000m²の手織りの絨毯がありこの絨毯にかけられた保険は ホテル全体のそれと同額という。ホテルは1957年に続き1978年に改装され 1974年にはフランス政府から歴史的建造物に指定されている。

開業/1978年(改装)　客室数/140室(内 スイート18室)　主な施設/宴会 会議場(最大1,000人収容)

各階を結ぶ階段　　The staircase connecting the floors.

HOTEL NEGRESCO

Facing the Promenade des Anglais in Nice, the largest city in Côte d'Azur, which is crowded with resort visitors, tourists, etc., the palace-like facade of "Hotel Negresco" serves as a landmark in Nice. For a long time, Nice has been visited by American multimillionaires, European Imperial Family members and nobles all year round. "Hotel Negresco" is a 4-star L high-class hotel founded in 1913 by Henri Negresco who was born in Rumania, with a view to realizing its concept; "a hotel suitable for such people."

All pieces of furniture, fixtures, tapestry, etc. are historical and luxurious, impressing us with the thoroughgoing collection spirit of conventional owners. In the "Salon Royal" in the center, there are chairs and round 2,000 m² homewoven carpet from the days of Louis XIV under the stained glass dome. The carpet is said to be insured for the same amount as that of the hotel as a whole. The hotel was refurbished in 1957 and 1978, and has been designated in 1974 by the French government as a historic building.

Opened/1978 (refurbished); Number of rooms/140 (including suite 18); Main facilities/banquet and conference rooms (capable of accommodating up to 1,000 persons).

上・下/サロン　各階段ごとに異なったスタイルで構成されている
Top・bottom / The salon; differs in style between the floors.

メイン ダイニング「Chantecler」　　　　　　　　　　The main dining "Chantecler."

バー　　　　　　　　　　The bar.

上・下／「Salon Louis XIV」　タペストリーは16世紀のもので　暖炉の重さは10tだという
Top・bottom / "Salon Louis XIV"; the tapestry dates back to the 16th century, and the fireplace is said to weigh 10 tons.

上・下／メリーゴーランド風のレストラン「La Rotonde」　　Top・bottom / The restaurant "La Rotonde" which looks like a merry-go-round.

スイートのリビング ルーム　　　　　　　　　　　　　　　　　　　　　　　　　　　　The suite's living room.

スイートのリビング ルーム　　　　　　　　　　　　　　　　　　　　　　　　　　　　The suite's living room.

スイートのベッド ルーム　　The suite's bedroom.	スイートのベッド ルーム　　The suite's bedroom.
スイートのベッド ルーム　　The suite's bedroom.	ジュニア スイートのベッド ルーム　　The junior suite's bedroom.
スイートの洗面台　　The suite's washstand.	スイートのバス ルーム　　The suite's bathroom.

吹抜け　5階からロビーを俯瞰する　　　　　　　　　　　　　　　The stairwell; overlooking the lobby from the 5th floor.

外観全景　　　　　The entire appearance.　　　　　レセプション　　　　　The reception.

The Ritz
PICCADILLY · LONDON

Add : Piccadilly, London W1. U.K.
Phone : 071-493-8181

レセプションからバー レストランへと続くロング ギャラリーをみる   The long gallery continuing from the reception to the bar and restaurant.

上・下/伝統的なアフタヌーン ティーとして有名な「Palm Court」　Top・bottom /"Palm Court" known for its traditional afternoon tea service.

「The Marie Antoinette Suite」 第二次大戦中チャーチル　アイゼンハワー　ド　ゴールの会談が行われたところ
"The Marie Antoinette Suite" where Churchill, Eisenhower and de Gaulle talked during the World War II.

「The Trafalga Suite」のダイニング　ルーム（20人用）　　　　　　　　　　The dining room (for 20 persons) of "The Trafalga Suite."

上・左下・右下／レストラン「The Restaurant」
Top・left, bottom・right, bottom / "The Restaurant."

ザ リッツ ロンドン

ロンドン ピカデリー(Piccadilly)にあり 西側にグリーン パークを一望できる五ツ星デラックス ホテル「The Ritz London」は 創始者であるCéser Ritzが今世紀初めに"世界の最もファッショナブルな都市における 最もファッショナブルなホテル"をコンセプトとして1906年に開業させたものである。インテリアはルイ16世調のフランス家具とデコレーションで統一され 数々の歴史的舞台として空間を提供してきた。マリー アントワネット スイートでは 第二次世界大戦中に チャーチル アイゼンハワー ド ゴールが何度か会談した 由緒あるプライベートサロンである。ロング ギャラリーの中間 左側の「パルム コート (Palm Court)」では 伝統的なアフタヌーン ティーでくつろげる。ウィーク エンドの夜にはライブ演奏があり '20〜'40年代のノスタルジックでタイムレスな雰囲気が楽しめる空間になっている。

開業/1979年(改装) 客室数/139室

スイートのリビング ルーム
The suite's living room.

THE RITZ LONDON

Situated at Piccadilly, London, "The Ritz London" is a 5-star deluxe hotel from which one can command a view of the Green Park on the west side. It was opened in 1906 by the founder Céser Ritz, with a view to realizing "the most fashionable hotel in the most fashionable city in the world" as a concept. The interior is united with pieces of French furniture and is decorated in the Louis XVI style, having served as the stage where a variety of historical dramas were played out. The "Marie Antoinette Suite" is a time-honored private salon where Churchill, General Eisenhower and General de Gaulle talked several times. On the left is the "Palm Court" in the center of the long gallery where guests can relax with a traditional afternoon tea. On weekend nights a live music is performed, and a nostalgic and timeless mood reminiscent of the 1920s to '40s can be enjoyed.

Opened/1979 (redecorated); Number of rooms/139.

左上/スイートのベッド ルーム
左下/スイートのバス ルーム
Left, top / The suite's bedroom.
Left, bottom / The suite's bathroom.

ドラゴン スタイルの木造の本館と手前の新館
The dragon-styled main wooden building and the new building on this side.

芝生のガーデンを通して本館東側をみる
The east side of the main building viewed across the grassed garden.

Holmenkollen Park Hotel Rica

Add : Kongeveien 26, N 0390 Oslo 3, Norway
Phone : 02-146090

ブルーと赤系のペイントはノルウェイの伝統色
The blue and reddish paints — traditional Norwegian colors.

ロビーから雪をイメージした彫刻を通してレセプションをみる
The reception viewed from the lobby across a piece of carving which images "snow."

2階からレセプションを俯瞰する
Overlooking the reception from the 2nd floor.

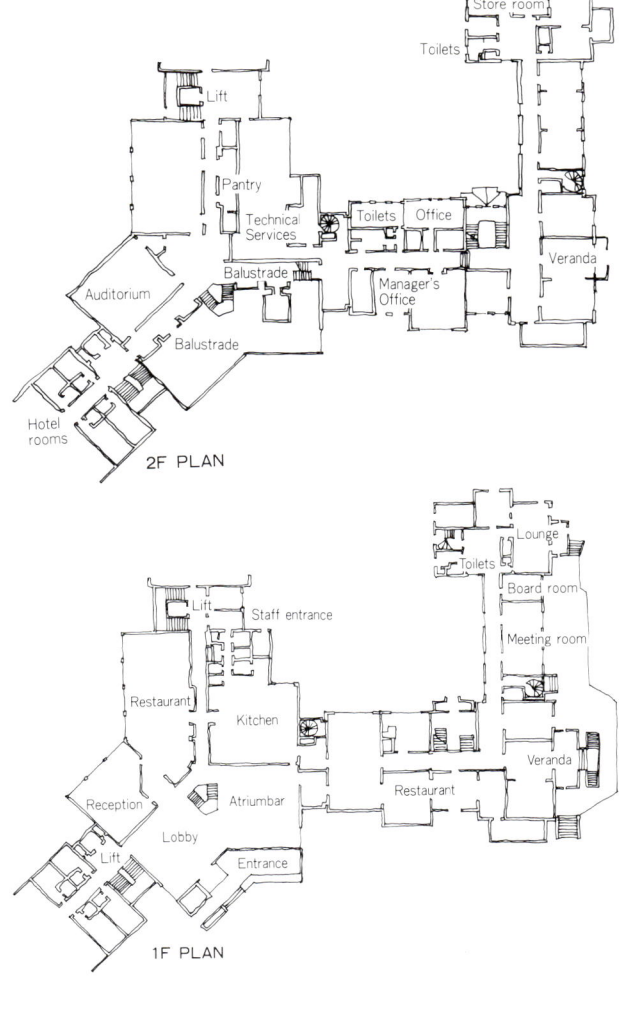

2F PLAN

1F PLAN

157

「Torjøn Falkanger」と「Arnfinn Bergman」とを合わせたコンファレンス ルーム
The conference room combining "Torjøn Falkanger" and "Arnfinn Bergman."

スキー スケートなど伝統的なスポーツ選手の記念写真が飾られている本館のコンシェルジュ
A concierge for the main building where souvenir photos of traditional sportsmen (skiing, skating, etc.) are displayed.

全体に彫刻が施された本館の階段廻り
The staircase area in the main building which is generally accented with carvings.

本館のコリドール

The corridor in the main building.

本館にあるレストラン

ホルメンコーレン パーク ホテル

「Holmenkollen Park Hotel」は スキー発祥の地ノルウェイの首都オスロの北西 世界的に有名なホルメンコーレン ジャンプ台のすぐ隣 海抜350mの高台に位置し オスロ フィヨルドの広大なパノラマと市街の全景の眺めが楽しめる。ホテルは 1894年に建造されたドラゴン スタイルのノルウェイ木造建築を復元した本館と1982年に増築されたモダンな新館で構成されている。ログと伝統的なタペストリー ペイント ハンド クラフトなどで装飾された「5つの部屋 (The Five Room)」と呼ばれるレストランのインテリアには ノルウェイ スタイルのバイキング料理や魚料理がマッチしている。コンベンション ルームには スキーの発祥地にふさわしく 国際的に活躍したスキーヤーなど スポーツ選手のポートレートが飾られている。ますます国際化が進み そのニーズに対応して現在400人収容可能なハイテックな2,800m²の会議場を建設中である。

開業/1982年(改装 増築) 客室数/200室 主な施設/宴会 会議場(会議170人 バンケット120人各収容可能 現在400人収容可能のハイテックな会議場を建設中)

HOLMENKOLLEN PARK HOTEL

The "Holmenkollen Park Hotel" stands on a hill 350 m above sea level, adjacent to the world-famous Holmenkollen ski jumping ground northwest of Oslo, the capital of Norway. Holmenkollen is the birthplace of skiing, and at the hotel guests can enjoy a panoramic view of the grand Oslo Fjord and the city.

The hotel is composed of the main building constructed by restoring the Norwegian dragon-style wooden structure built in 1894 to its original state, plus the modern new building which was extended in 1982. The interior of the restaurant is called "The Five Room" and is decorated with logs, traditional tapestry, paint, handicrafts, etc., and matches well with Norwegian smorgasbord, fish dishes,

ランチ時のテーブル セッティング
Table setting at lunchtime.

The restaurant in the main building.

ログ タペストリー 時計などがうまく調和しているコーナー
A corner where logs, tapestry, clocks, etc. are harmoniously placed.

海の幸が豊富なバイキング スタイル
The smorgasbord style featuring a variety of marine products.

etc. The convention room is decorated with portraits of skiers and other sportsmen who are internationally well known – a feature becoming to the birthplace of skiing. In order to respond to the increasing needs for a convention space reflecting the rapid internationalization, the hotel is currently constructing a high tech 2 800 m² convention room capable of accommodating up to 400 persons.

Opened/1982 (redecorated/extended); Number of rooms/200; Main facilities/banquet and conference rooms (capable of accommodating 170 persons in the conference space and 120 persons in the banquet space): at present, a high tech convention room (capable of accommodating up to 400 persons) is under construction.

2階からバー エリアを俯瞰する

Overlooking the bar area from the 2nd floor.

ロビーの一角にあるバー

The bar occupying a corner of the lobby.

1780年に建造された穀物倉庫を改装した「アドミラル ホテル」
"Admiral Hotel" built by refurbishing a granary which was constructed in 1780.

両サイドのエントランス前に置かれた二門の大砲
The two guns placed in front of the right- and left-hand entrances.

ファサード
The facade.

Copenhagen Admiral Hotel

Add : Toldbodgade 24-28, DK-1253 Copenhagen K, Denmark
Phone : 33-118282

コペンハーゲン アドミラル ホテル
このホテルは 18世紀の穀物倉庫を改装し 1978年に開業したデンマークの国際級ホテルである。コペンハーゲンとオスロ間をクルーズする 豪華船の発着埠頭となっている運河に面して建っている。構造となっているパイン材の柱と梁を骨格にして ブロック クリンカー(brick clinker) 木を仕上げ材に使用し スティール コンクリート材は避け 機能的な北欧の暖かい空間をつくりあげているのが特徴である。アマリエンボーグ(Amalienborg)宮殿にも近く ゲイフォンの噴水(Geifon fountain)や 人魚姫の像(The Little Mermaid) 運河沿いの散策には 立地的に絶好のホテルである。ホテル名になっているアドミラル(Admiral－海軍大将)にちなんで エントランスにはクラシックな二門の大砲が置かれており 金曜日の午後には号砲も聞かれる。デンマーク人らしい室内空間の快適さを表現したホテルといえる。
開業/1978年 客室数/366室(シングル9室 ダブル305室 ジュニア スイート46室 シニア スイート6室) 主な施設/宴会 会議場(最大500人収容可能)

COPENHAGEN ADMIRAL HOTEL

Opened in 1978 by refurbishing an 18th century granary, the "Copenhagen Admiral Hotel" is a Danish hotel in the international class. It faces a canal where deluxe cruisers cruising between Copenhagen and Oslo arrive/depart. Based on pine pillars and beams as the framing members, the structure is finished with brick clinkers and wood; steel and concrete are avoided thereby creating a functional but warm Scandinavian atmosphere. Close to the Amalienborg, there are the Geifon Fountain and The Little Mermaid, so that the hotel gives guests a golden opportunity to walk along the canal. In association with the name which contains "Admiral," the entrance is accented with two classic guns, and on Friday afternoons guests can hear the gun shots. The hotel may be said to be expressing a comfortable indoor space local to Denmark.

Opened/1978; Number of rooms/366 (single 9, double 305, junior suite 46, senior suite 6); Main facilities/banquet and conference rooms (max. capacity is 500 persons).

200年以上も前の柱や梁を使用したレセプション
The reception utilizing the pillars and beams which were placed more than 200 years ago.

右上/エントランス奥にあるレストランへのアプローチ
右下/エントランスからロビーをみる 船に因んだインテリアが多い

Right, top / The approach to the restaurant at the back of the restaurant.
Right, bottom / The lobby viewed from the entrance; the interior uses a lot of ship-related items.

バーからレセプション方向をみる　　　The reception area viewed from the bar.

船首の装飾　The bow decoration.

バーカウンター　　　The bar counter.

上／デンマークのオープン サンド（スモアーブロ）
　　セルフサービスする
下／テーブル セッティング

Top / Danish open sandwich (self-service).
Bottom / Table setting.

木の梁を通してレストランを俯瞰する

Overlooking the restaurant through wooden beams.

レストラン　昼はデンマーク式バイキング

The restaurant; Danish smorgasbord in the daytime.

ナイト クラブ　　　The night club.

人魚の像　　　　The mermaid statue.　　　　テーブル席　　　　Table seating.

ベッドからリビング ルームを俯瞰する
Overlooking the living room from the bed.

ツイン ルーム(スタンダード)
The twin room (standard).

北欧のモダン家具を配したリビング ルーム
The living room featuring modern Scandinavian furniture.

BONAPARTE HOTEL

Add : Via De Amicis 32, 20123 Milano, Italy
Phone : 2-72000581

ボナパルト ホテル

デザイン ファッション ビジネスでフィーバーするミラノ 数多くあるミラノのホテルの中で 最もプライバシーが尊重されているのがこの「ボナパルト ホテル」であろう。アミシス通り(Via de Amicis)に面した住宅 小売店などがひしめく建物の前面に位置し ファサードには大きなキャノピーが設けられており フロントは ロータリーとなっている。インテリアは モダーン及びモダーン クラシックで統一されていて 落ち着いている。レストラン カフェ バー ピアノ バーはホーム リビングを延長させたような 家庭的な雰囲気が漂う。地下には洞窟状のレンガ造りのバー プライベート ルームがあり 小人数のパーティーに最適である。客室には インフォメーション セキュリティー システムの端末があり ドア サイドに表示され プライバシーは 最大限に守られている。

客室数/52室(内 スイート ルーム6室)

BONAPARTE HOTEL

Milano is boiling with the design and fashion business. It may be said that the "Bonaparte Hotel," among many hotels in Milano, pays the highest regard for privacy. Facing a building along Via de Amicis which is jammed with residences, retail stores, etc., the hotel's facade features a large canopy and the front is rotary. The interior is finished with modern or modern-classic design and has a composed atmosphere. The restaurant, cafe bar and piano bar is filled with a homely atmosphere, as if a home living space has been extended. Under ground are a bricked, cave-like bar and private rooms which are most suitable for small parties. Each guest room has a terminal of an information security system which displays information on the door side, thereby protecting privacy to the utmost.

Number of rooms/52 (including suite 6).

市の中心部にあるホテル   The hotel situated in the center of the city.

キャノピーのディテール
The canopy in details.

キャノピーでアプローチ
The canopied approach.

ロビー ラウンジ
The lobby lounge.

レセプション
The reception.

エレベーター前からロビー方向をみる
The lobby area viewed from the elevator.

バー ラウンジ
The bar lounge.

地下のバーにある会議室に下りる階段廻り
The area around the staircase leading to the conference room within the underground bar.

地下の会議室にあるバー カウンター
The bar counter in the underground conference room.

ジュニア スイートのベッド ルーム
The junior suite's bedroom.

左上/ジュニア スイートのデスク
左下/ドア サイドのセキュリティー インフォメーション システム
右上/ジュニア スイートのバス ルーム

Left, top / The junior suite's desk.
Left, bottom / The security information system on the door side.
Right, top / The junior suite's bathroom.

モンテーニュ大通り (Avenue Montaigne) に面するホテルのファサード
The hotel's facade facing the Avenue Montaigne.

ロビーを通してレセプションをみる
The reception viewed across the lobby.

PLAZA ATHÉNÉE
Add : 25 Avenue Montaigne 75008 Paris, France
Phone : 1-47 23 78 33

ロビー
The lobby.

ガーデンを俯瞰する
Overlooking the garden.

右/ガーデン レストラン
Right / The garden restaurant.

オテル プラザ アテネ

パリの高級ファッション ブティックが集まるモンテーニュ大通り(Avenue Montaigne)にある「Hôtel Plaza Athénée」は ロビー レストラン ギャラリー 客室 レセプション コンベンション ルームに至るまで 豪華さと優雅さを売り物にしている四ツ星デラックスホテルである。ルイ16世調の家具のレストラン「Regence」と'30年代のデコ スタイルの「Le Relais Plaza」 アフタヌーン ティーのゆったりしたギャラリーは パリの余裕を持った伝統が生きている感じである。このホテルには 花が多く飾られているのが特徴で 花にかける費用がホテルの光熱費を上回るという。旅人をやさしく迎え入れようという 長年のポリシーが徹底している証しであろう。また一室あたり従業員2人というサービスも充実している。春から秋にかけては中庭に「ダイニング コート (Dining Court)」がオープン。紅いパラソルやテントが壁面を覆う蔦に映えて鮮やかである。ワインセラーにはホテルやレストランを利用する紳士 淑女のために 常時10万本のワインがストックされている。

開業/1912年 客室数/218室(内 スイート44室)

HÔTEL PLAZA ATHÉNÉE

Standing by the Avenue Montaigne where high class fashion boutiques in Paris are open in a row, the "Hôtel Plaza Athénée" is a 4-star deluxe hotel featuring gorgeousness and elegance in the lobby, restaurant, gallery, guest rooms, reception and convention rooms. The restaurant "Regence" is in the Louis XVI style, "Le Relais Plaza" in the '30s deco style, and the spacious gallery where guests can enjoy an afternoon tea – one can feel that a dignified Parisian tradition is still alive. The hotel is characterized by a lot of decorative flowers whose cost is said to be higher than the total cost of light and fuel. It seems to be proof of many years' policy for warmly welcoming travellers. Two employees are assigned to each room to provide the best service. From spring to autumn, the "Dining Court" opens on the courtyard. Red parasols and tents vividly contrast with an ivy-covered wall. In the wine cellar there are always 100,000 bottles of wine for ladies and gentlemen who utilize the hotel and restaurant.

Opened/1912; Number of rooms/218 (including suite 44).

右上/レストラン「Regence」
右下/「Regence」ルイ16世調の豪華さ
Right, top / The restaurant "Regence."
Right, bottom / "Regence"; gorgeousness in the Louis XVI style.

サロン「Montaigne」 カクテル パーティ プライベイト ディナー 会議などに使用
The salon "Montaigne"; used for a cocktail party, private dinner, conference, etc.

左/サロン「Marie Artoinette」 最高100人までの会議が可能
上/レストラン「Le Relais Plaza」 1930年代のデコ スタイル

Left / The salon "Marie Artoinette"; capable of accommodating up to 100 persons.
Top / The restaurant "Le Relais Plaza"; the 1930s deco style.

スイートのリビング ルーム　　The suite's living room.

スイートのベッド ルーム　　The suite's bedroom.

スイートのリビング ルーム — The suite's living room.

暖炉の上の置時計 — A clock on the fireplace.

エレガントなカーテンと家具 — The elegant curtain and furniture.

コースを通して外観全景をみる

The entire appearance viewed across the course.

メイン エントランス — The main entrance.

プロ ショップ側のファサード — The facade on the pro shop side.

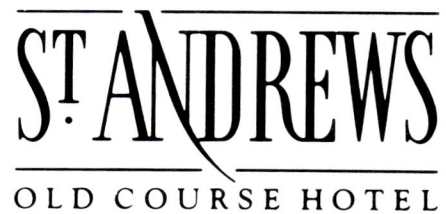

ST ANDREWS
OLD COURSE HOTEL

Add : St.Andrews, Fife, Scotland, U.K.
Phone : 0334-74371

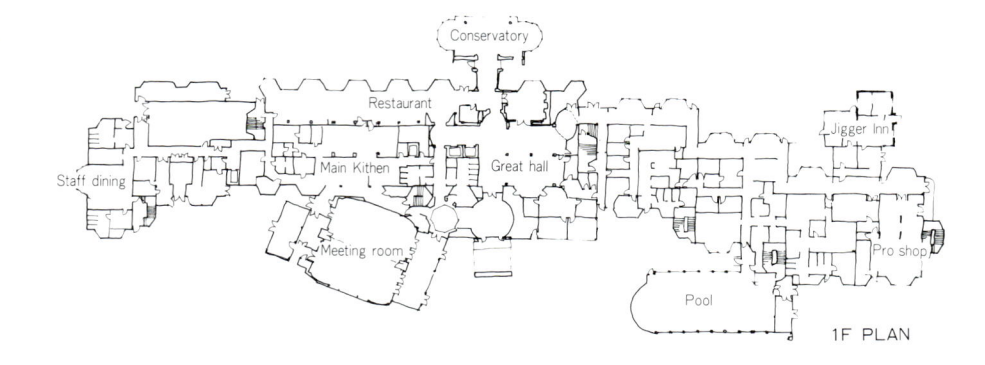

1F PLAN

エントランス サイドのフォイヤー（Foyer＝玄関の広間）

The foyer (entrance hall) on the entrance side.

エレベーター前からロビーをみる
The lobby viewed from the elevator.

「The Liblary」　棚の上のペインティングが独特
"The Library"; accented with unique paintings on the shelves.

オールド コースのレストラン「Road Hole Grill」　　　　The restaurant "Road Hole Grill" on the old course.

温室を思わせるレストラン「The Conservatory」　　　　　The restaurant "The Conservatory" reminiscent of a hothouse.

コテージ バー「Jigger Inn」
The cottage bar "Jigger Inn."

バー カウンター　　The bar counter.

セント アンドリュース オールド コース ホテル

世界的に有名なゴルフのセント アンドリュース オールド コースの17番フェア ウエイを見下ろす場所に建つこのホテルは　サンドストーンのファサードが　海岸コースの平坦な芝生のグリーンによく映える。1968年の開業であるが　これまでに数多くのプレイヤーやゴルフ関係者に　宿泊とスコットランドのホスピタリティーを提供してきた。又このホテルはゴルフに限らず　乗馬　ハンティング　フィッシングなどアウトドア スポーツのオプション基地としてもトップクラスのサービスを提供している。

開業/1968年

ST. ANDREWS OLD COURSE HOTEL

Overlooking the #17 fairway of the world-famous St. Andrews Old Course, the hotel features the sandstone facade which vividly stands out against the flat coastal course. Since its opening in 1968, the hotel has furnished many players and those involved in golf with comfortable lodging and Scottish hospitality. It also offers top-class services as an outdoor sports option station not merely for golf but also horse riding, hunting, fishing, etc.

Opened/1968.

スイートのリビング ルーム

The suite's living room.

デスクからベッド ルームをみる

The bedroom viewed from the desk.

スイートのベッド ルーム　　　　　　　　　　　　　　　　　　　　　　　　　　　The suite's bedroom.

ソファのディテール　　The sofa in details.

フラワー アレンジメント　　Flower arrangements.

クラッシックな机と椅子　　The classic desk and chairs.

「Salon Spa」のプール

The pool of "Salon Spa."

「Salon Spa」のレセプション
The reception of "Salon Spa."

プロ ショップ前のコリドールにある歴代の優勝者の名前を刻んだボード
The names of successive champions are inscribed on the board along the corridor of the pro shop.

レセプションから「The Promenard」へのホールを見上げる   The hall leading to "The Promenade" looked up at from the reception.

THE DORCHESTER
Add　: Park Lane London W1, U.K.
Phone : 071-629-8888

ファサード   The facade.

ザ ドルチェスター

ロンドンのメイフェア(Mayfair)地区にあるこの「The Dorchester」からは ハイド パーク(Hyde Park)が見下ろせる。1931年に開業して以来 各界から人気を得た五ツ星デラックスホテルで 第二次世界大戦中 アイゼンハワー将軍は ノルマンディ上陸作戦にあたって ここを作戦本部にしていたこともある。1990年11月の大がかりな増 改築を経て 現在に至っている。レセプション フロアから続いて アフターヌーン ティーの「The Promenade」 メイン ダイニングの英国料理「The Grill Room」 レストラン「The Terrace」 バー「The Bar」 メンバーズ クラブ「The Dorchester Club」 広東料理レストラン「The Oriental」などの料飲施設があり 特に「The Bar」は1938年のオープン以来 ロンドンの高級なミーティング ポイントとして知られ 今も利用されている。
開業/1990年(改装) 客室数/252室(ツイン197室 スイート55室) 主な施設/宴会 会議場(最大800人収容 カクテル パーティーは1,000人収容可能) スパ ヘルス クラブ

THE DORCHESTER

From "The Dorchester" in Mayfair, London, guests can command a view of Hyde Park. Since its opening in 1931 as a 5-star deluxe hotel, it has become popular with various people. During World War II, General Eisenhower used the hotel as the headquarters for the Normandy landing. In November 1990 it went through extensive refurbishment. From the reception floor one enters the eating & drinking space comprising "The Promenade" for afternoon tea, main dining "The Grill Room" serving English dishes, restaurant "The Terrace," "The Bar," the members club "The Dorchester Club," Kwangtung restaurant "The Oriental," etc. Since its opening in 1938, "The Bar," among others, has been known as a high-class meeting point in London and is still utilized.

Opened/1990 (refurbished); Number of rooms/252 (twin 197, suite 55); Main facilities/banquet and conference rooms (capable of accommodating up to 800 persons; a cocktail party can accommodate up to 1,000 persons), spa, health club.

レセプション ホール　　The reception hall.

レセプション サイドからキャッシャー方向をみる　　The cashier area viewed from the reception side.

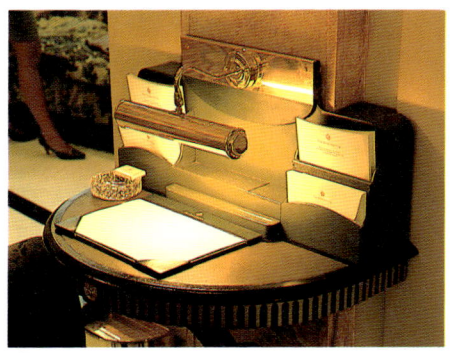

ゲスト用デスク　　The desk for guests.

メザニン階のギャラリー　　The gallery on the mezzanine floor.

ホテルの中央に位置するアフタヌーン ティーの「The Promenade」
"The Promenade" in the center of the hotel where one can taste a cup of afternoon tea.

「The Promenade」からレストラン「The Terrace」をみる
The restaurant "The Terrace" viewed from "The Promenade."

上・下／メイン レストラン「The Grill Room」　　　　　　　　　　　　　Top・bottom / The main restaurant "The Grill Room."

「The Bar」壁面のセラミックはフランス人Alberto Pinto氏の作品
"The Bar"; The ceramic on the wall was produced by Alberto Pinto, a French artist.

Alberto Pinto氏がデザインした「The Terrace」
"The Terrace" designed by Alberto Pinto.

スイートのベッド ルーム　　　　　　　　　　　　　　　　　　　　　　　　　　　The suite's bedroom.

左/TVもクラシックなデザイン
Left / TV also features a classic design.

スイートのダイニング ルーム　　The suite's dining room.

バス ルーム　　The bathroom.

王宮側から外観全景をみる — The entire appearance viewed from the Royal Palace side.

ドアマン — A doorman.

ロビー 右側がレセプション — The lobby; with the reception on the right side.

GRAND HÔTEL

Add : S.Blasieholmhamnen 8, P.O.Box 16424, S-10327 Stockholm, Sweden
Phone : 08-221020

ロビー サロン

The lobby salon.

グランド ホテル ストックホルム

王宮を目の前に望めるストックホルムの一等地にあるこの「GRAND HOTEL STOCKHOLM」は 国立博物館 オペラ(Operan)劇場やドラマーテン劇場(Dramatiska Teatern) ガムラ スターン (Gamla Stan)と呼ばれる旧市街などに近く 観光的に便利な場所に位置している。ホテル前には 群島巡りの観光船の発着場がある。インテリアは伝統的な北欧エレガンスと格調の高さを誇り 最近改装されたモダンな客室 カーテンやベッドなどと アンティークな調度品がうまく調和している。カフェ バーやフレンチ レストランのテラス サイドからはパノラマが展開し 王宮や湾内に浮かぶ帆船 連絡船などを眺めながら食事やティー タイムを楽しめる。質 眺めとも ウォーター フロントにおける最も豪華なホテルになっている。

主な施設/宴会 会議場(20室 最大700人収容)

GRAND HOTEL STOCKHOLM

The "Grand Hotel Stockholm" stands on the first-class quarter in Stockholm just facing the Royal Palace. In its vicinity there are the National Museum, Operan (i.e. Opera) Theater, Dramatiska Teatern (i.e. Dramatic Theater), etc. There also is an old street called Gamla Stan. Thus, the hotel is conveniently situated for sightseeing. In front of the hotel, there is a landing place where sightseeing boats, which cruise around a group of islands, arrive and depart. The interior features traditional Scandinavian elegance and a dignified appearance, harmoniously placing guest rooms which have been recently modernized, curtains, beds, etc., with pieces of antique furniture. From the terrace side of the cafe bar or French restaurant guests can command a panoramic view of the Royal Palace, sailing boats floating on the bay, ferryboats, etc., while enjoying eating or drinking a cup of tea. Thus, in both quality and view, the "Grand Hotel Stockholm" is the most gorgeous hotel on the waterfront.

Main facilities/banquet and conference rooms (20 rooms – capable of accommodating up to 700 persons).

入口

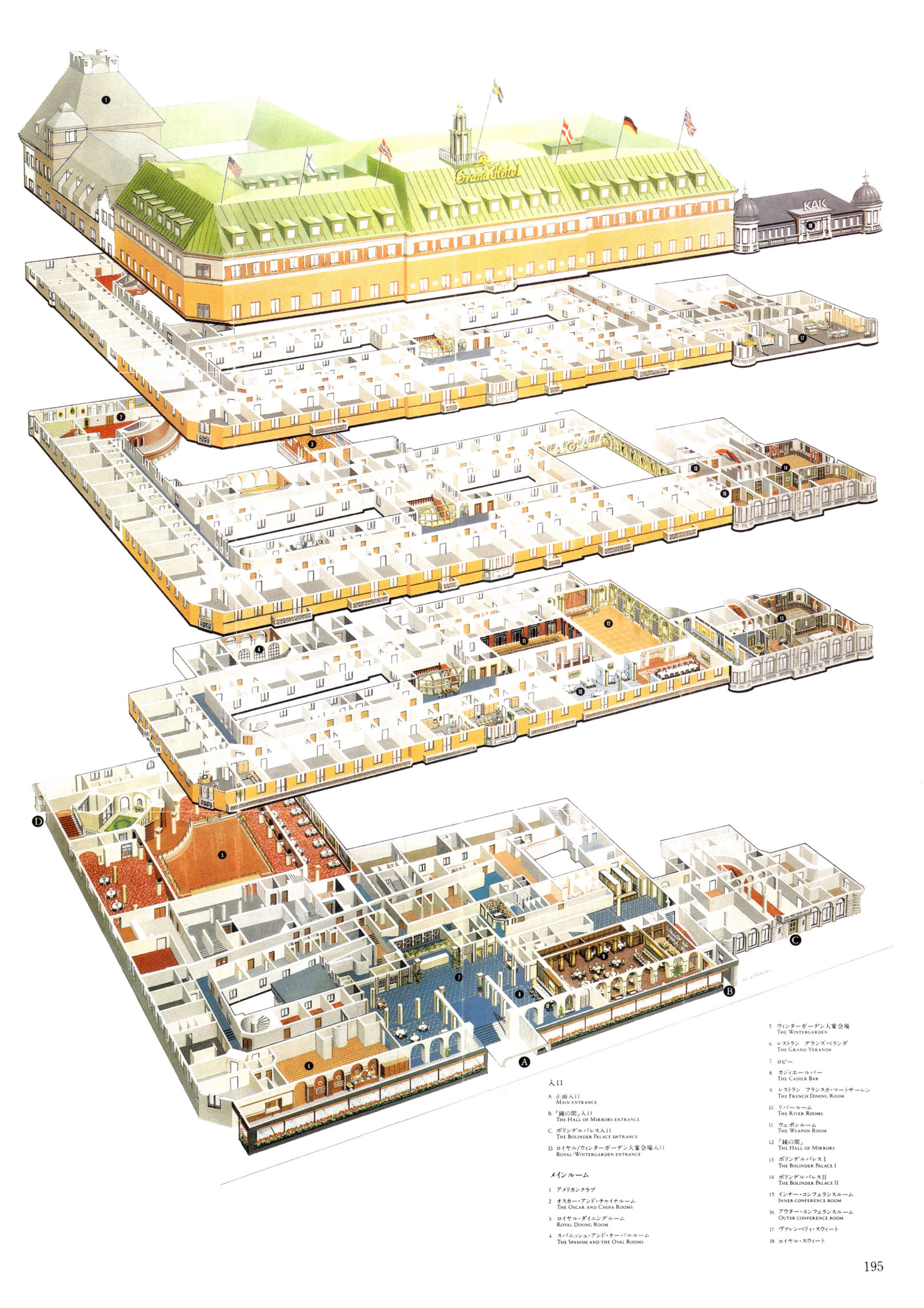

A. 正面入口
   Main entrance
B. 「鏡の間」入口
   The Hall of Mirrors entrance
C. ボリンデルパレス入口
   The Bolinder Palace entrance
D. ロイヤル/ウィンターガーデン大宴会場入口
   Royal/Wintergarden entrance

メインルーム

1. アメリカンクラブ
2. オスカー・アンド・チャイナルーム
   The Oscar and China Rooms
3. ロイヤル・ダイニングルーム
   Royal Dining Room
4. スパニッシュ・アンド・オーバルルーム
   The Spanish and the Oval Rooms
5. ウィンターガーデン大宴会場
   The Wintergarden
6. レストラン グランズベランダ
   The Grand Veranda
7. ロビー
8. カジィエールバー
   The Cadier Bar
9. レストラン フランスカ・マートサーレン
   The French Dining Room
10. リバールーム
    The River Rooms
11. ウェポンルーム
    The Weapon Room
12. 「鏡の間」
    The Hall of Mirrors
13. ボリンデルパレス I
    The Bolinder Palace I
14. ボリンデルパレス II
    The Bolinder Palace II
15. インナー・コンフェランスルーム
    Inner conference room
16. アウター・コンフェランスルーム
    Outer conference room
17. ヴァレンベリ・スウィート
18. ロイヤル・スウィート

195

「Grand Cafe」 王宮を眺めながらスウェーデン料理が楽しめる
"Grand Café"; guests can enjoy Swedish delicacies, while viewing the Royal Palace.

明るいテラスはリラックス ムード
On the bright terrace guests feel relaxed.

上・左下／レストラン「The French Dining Room」　　　　　　　　　Top · left, bottom / The restaurant "The French Dining Room."

テーブル セッティング　　　Table setting

大宴会場「The Winter Garden」のテーブル セッティング　　Table setting for the large banquet hall "The Winter Garden."

「The Winter Garden」は900m²の広さを持つ　　"The Winter Garden" has 900 m² of space.

「The Cadier Bar」のテラス　河の向かい側に王宮が眺められる
The terrace of "The Cadier Bar"; guests can command a view of the Royal Palace on the other side of the river.

左／バー カウンター
Left / The bar counter.

スイートのリビング ルーム

The suite's living room.

エレガントなカーテンと家具
The elegant curtain and furniture.

モダンなベッド
The modern bed.